Mystery of the Kingdom of
HEAVEN

DEBORAH BOUCHARD

WESTBOW
PRESS
A DIVISION OF THOMAS NELSON
& ZONDERVAN

Copyright © 2014 Deborah Bouchard.

All rights reserved. No part of this book may be used or reproduced by any means, graphic, electronic, or mechanical, including photocopying, recording, taping or by any information storage retrieval system without the written permission of the publisher except in the case of brief quotations embodied in critical articles and reviews.

Scripture taken from the New King James Version. Copyright © 1979, 1980, 1982 by Thomas Nelson, Inc. Used by permission. All rights reserved.

WestBow Press books may be ordered through booksellers or by contacting:

WestBow Press
A Division of Thomas Nelson & Zondervan
1663 Liberty Drive
Bloomington, IN 47403
www.westbowpress.com
1 (866) 928-1240

Because of the dynamic nature of the Internet, any web addresses or links contained in this book may have changed since publication and may no longer be valid. The views expressed in this work are solely those of the author and do not necessarily reflect the views of the publisher, and the publisher hereby disclaims any responsibility for them.

Any people depicted in stock imagery provided by Thinkstock are models, and such images are being used for illustrative purposes only. Certain stock imagery © Thinkstock.

ISBN: 978-1-4908-6219-4 (sc)
ISBN: 978-1-4908-6221-7 (hc)
ISBN: 978-1-4908-6220-0 (e)

Library of Congress Control Number: 2014921555

Printed in the United States of America.

WestBow Press rev. date: 12/12/2014

All Bible Reference used in this
book has come from:

New King James Version
"Spirit Filled Life Bible"
Thomas Nelson Publishers, Nashville
Copyright 1991 by Thomas Nelson, Inc.

The Holy Bible, New King James Version
Copyright 1982 by Thomas Nelson, Inc.

The New King James Bible, New Testament
Copyright 1979 by Thomas Nelson, Inc.

The New King James Bible, New
Testament and Psalms
Copyright 1980 by Thomas Nelson, Inc.

Also some scripture was paraphrased to place
the story in a more current context. Some stories
required a collaboration of several accounts from
the Gospels that helped make the story flow.

Dedication

I want to thank the Lord, my God for bringing this story to us through His Holy Word, the Bible. Then my deep appreciation goes to those men and women who have taught me how to interpret scriptures and brought a deeper understanding of the intent of God's precious message.

To Perry Stone whose ministry inspired me through tapes and conferences. To Rhema Bible College and Kenneth E. Hagin whose books and tapes also fed me rich and deep understanding of God's love and purpose for my life.

To Pastors Todd and Karen Smith who motivated me to move from a simple pew-sitting believer to a soldier in the army of God. Also for daring to start a Bible school to teach me how to advance in the Kingdom. It was through their ministry that I was able to travel to multiple nations to experience other cultures and to develop a passion for missions.

I also dedicate this book to the men who poured knowledge into me. To the late Dr. Miles Munroe whose books on the Kingdom of Heaven have inspired me to search truths beyond this world. Thanks to, Dr. Ed Kuhn, for his deep knowledge of practical theology and great patience while teaching the deep mysteries of God. My deepest thanks and appreciation to Pastor Robin Martin for his dedication and passion for the message of healing and faith. Also for allowing me to walk by his side as he ministered while I learned how to let the Holy Spirit in me minister to the sick and tormented.

I also dedicate this book to my parents, Dwight and Tich Cook who raised me in a Christian home giving me the love and nurturing that brought me to the place where I accepted Jesus Christ as my Savior.

Lastly, without the love, support and encouragement of my husband, Bob, I would have never experienced the international travel and experiences that have led me to the place of writing this book. Without that travel, I would never have seen those living in developing nations who needed a deeper understanding of the nature of God and His love for *all* people and nations.

Contents

Introduction xi

1. The Beginning 1
2. The Garden 5
3. Lost Dominion 9
4. The Kingdom Re-Enters the Earth 15
5. Thy Kingdom Come 19
6. The Decree 25
7. Jesus Meets Cousin John 33
8. Jesus Meets Satan 39
9. Jesus Returns to His Hometown 45
10. Jesus Ministers to the Hopeless 49
11. Jesus and His Disciples 53
12. The Blind Can See 55
13. Boy Delivered from Demonic Spirits 61
14. You Must Be Born Again 65
15. Don't Worry 71
16. Jesus and the Parables 75
17. A Few Loaves and Fish Feed Thousands 81
18. Moved by Faith 85
19. The Day of Great Miracles 89
20. The Religious System 95
21. Power of Binding and Loosing 99
22. Learning To Pray 103
23. Understanding Who Jesus Is 107
24. Jesus Is The Only Way 113

25.	Enemies of Jesus	121
26.	Jesus' View of Wealth	125
27.	Jesus and the Death of Lazarus	129
28.	Satan's Plot to Remove Jesus	135
29.	Darkness Closes In	137
30.	The Triumphal Entry	139
31.	More to Teach	143
32.	Jesus Celebrates Passover with His Disciples	147
33.	A New Covenant	151
34.	The Holy Spirit Revealed	155
35.	Final Instructions	159
36.	The Coming of the Holy Spirit	161
37.	Jesus Asks God to Deliver Him From This Hour	165
38.	Trial and Denial	169
39.	Rome Tries Jesus	173
40.	Pilate Sentences Jesus	177
41.	The Cross	181
42.	The Death of Jesus	187
43.	The Keys Regained	193
44.	Jesus Lives	199
45.	Jesus Appears In Person	205
46.	The 40-Day Walk	211

Epilogue 219
Author's Note 221
The Mystery Answered 223

Introduction

I have been traveling to nations on four continents for over fifteen years and enjoy the people in every area I visit. The more I visited villages and towns in these countries, I felt a burden developing in me. I realized that the gospel of Jesus wasn't completely understood or it had been changed to fit certain religious practices. I also felt that there was a depth to the message of the life of Jesus that was missing as the people were being discipled. I realized that we who are comfortable with "churchy" words include them in our conversation, but the meanings are not understood. For that reason, I included boxes of words with their definitions.

Several years ago, I discovered a new way to understand the message about the Kingdom of Heaven and knew that there was a mystery that was being revealed to me. At various intervals in *The Mystery of the Kingdom of Heaven*, you will see a picture of keys. Keys are a symbol of power and authority in the natural world. The same goes with the spiritual. The journey of the keys started in the Garden of Eden and has traveled in time to Jesus. Through Jesus' death, burial and resurrection those keys have been passed on to us. We now hold the keys of power and authority over the enemy of our souls, Satan.

As you read this book, you will walk through time from the Garden to the resurrection of Jesus. His life was a sacrifice for you and which now gives us the keys. Those keys of power are for every believer and can give you a life of victory on this side of heaven.

It is my desire that we realize the sacrifice Jesus made so we can exert our power and authority over our enemy, Satan.

The Kingdom of Heaven
The Mystery

...to make all see what is the fellowship of the mystery, which from the beginning of the ages has been hidden in God who created all things through Jesus Christ. Ephesians 3:9

CHAPTER 1

The Beginning

Lucifer was a magnificent angel, beautiful in every way. He was in the same league with Michael, the archangel and Gabriel, the messenger. He held the rank of captain and did his tasks well. There was a song in him that drew others to sing praises to God. Even God called him the light-bringer and son of the morning.

But Lucifer's beauty began to consume him, and he thought more about himself than the God he served. He began to think that he could possibly gain more popularity with the lesser angels and even outrank God. Lucifer let his pride develop until, one day, he challenged Jehovah God.

On that momentous day, Lucifer had hardened his heart toward El Elyon, the Most High God. He believed that he could do a better job, be more efficient than God, and take control over all the elements that held the universe. His thoughts about taking dominion were so strong, that they made him act and speak differently. The Lord knew what was in Lucifer's heart because God knows all things; He is omniscient.

The Lord said to Lucifer, "You have said in your heart: I will ascend into heaven and I will exalt my throne above the stars of God; I will also sit on the mount of the congregation on the farthest sides of the north. I will ascend above the heights of the clouds, and I will be like the Most High." (Isaiah 14:13-14)

God continued, "Lucifer you will never reach the height of My kingdom and you will never rule above me. For your wicked ambitions, I will cast you out of this kingdom and you will ultimately be condemned to the lowest depths of the pit."

With that, Lucifer was cast out of the Kingdom of heaven not with the accolades or applause of those who served in heaven, but with rejection and condemnation.

Before he left, Lucifer was able to collect one-third of the angels in the kingdom and take them with him to serve him in his new world, Earth. Lucifer lost his title, position, and good name when he was expelled from the heavenly kingdom. He became known as Satan or the Devil, and his fallen angels became known as demons. No longer were they happy and full of music but now full of pride, anger, resentment, murder, and lust - for more of anything they could get. They also hated all of mankind. God no longer loved and cherished Lucifer because he was full of self-pride. Never would he be accepted back into the Kingdom of God.

God, the King of heaven remains as the Most High. There is no other god higher than Him. Satan is now His enemy and dwells on the earth to be a menace. Satan's whole purpose is to kill, steal and destroy mankind. He does this through deception, lies, and manipulation.

You may ask, "Why does Satan hate humans so much?" In the scriptures, it is written that God created man in His image. Every time Satan sees a human, he wants to destroy that person because he reminds Satan of God.

CHAPTER 2

The Garden

It was a perfect environment on Earth, with lush green plants that provided the perfect place for beautiful animals and creatures to live. It was called the Garden of Eden. God had created the garden as a sanctuary of peace and perfect health for its inhabitants. There was no sickness, food was ample, water was clear and clean, and everything lived in harmony. This was God's Paradise.

God was proud of His creations. Each creature was unique, and Jehovah had fun creating each one. They were perfect in every way.

One day, the Lord God was walking in the garden communing with the man He had created. Adam was the crown of all His achievements. God empowered Adam by saying, "Be fruitful and multiply; fill the earth and subdue it; have

The Garden

dominion over the fish of the sea, over the birds of the air, and over every living thing that moves on the earth." (Gen. 1:28) Adam understood that God had authorized him to govern the earth. He was to manage, lead, and rule, for he was in God's kingdom on the Earth. God was giving Adam the keys to His kingdom.

> **Keys**
> *A symbol of power and authority*

God continued to walk with Adam, explaining the reason the man was there. First and foremost, Adam was God's friend. Jehovah God clearly described the role Adam would play; to maintain dominion and keep God's perfect garden. God took the man, and together they looked over the beauty God had formed. Every tree was pleasant to the sight and good for food. The Tree of Life was in the midst of the garden, as well as the Tree of the Knowledge of Good and Evil. (Gen. 2:9) The Lord said, "See all these trees and plants? You may eat anything from them, but of that tree." The Lord pointed, "That one contains the knowledge of good and evil and you shall not eat from it. If you do, that day you will die" (Gen. 2:16-17). Adam nodded

> **Dominion**
> *Prevail against, reign, rule over, dominate*

soberly, understanding the severity of God's command.

The Lord gave Adam an assignment to exercise his creative side. Adam was to give a name to every creature on the land, every beast of the field and every bird of the air and every fish in the sea. (Gen. 2:19) While Adam was busy creating names, God looked over His creations and then at the man. He said, "It is not good that man should be alone; I will make him a helper that is much like him" (Gen. 2:18).

One day, God caused a deep sleep to come over Adam. While in that sleep, God took a rib from Adam's side and fashioned another human, a woman with the name Eve (Gen. 2:21-22). The man and woman lived in the beautiful garden and God gave them dominion, or total charge, over everything that lived. The woman, Eve, was Adam's help-mate, for she completed him in every way. They shared ideas and worked together, for the Lord had created them to work side by side.

CHAPTER 3

Lost Dominion

Adam and Eve lived in the garden, enjoying communion with the animals, and eating delicious food provided by the garden. In the evenings they walked and talked with their Maker, the Lord God. It was a beautiful existence that would soon be shattered.

One day, Lucifer appeared to Eve disguised as a serpent. With great cunning he came to trick her into being disobedient to God's command not to eat from the Tree of the Knowledge of Good and Evil. Adam was given that directive when it was only he that lived in the garden. Adam told Eve what God said when she became a part of his life.

Knowing that Eve had heard this important commandment second hand, Satan didn't have much trouble confusing her. He said, "You shall not eat of every tree of the garden?" (Gen. 3:1).

Eve replied, "We may eat the fruit of the trees of the garden; but of the fruit of the tree which is in the midst of the garden, God has said, 'You shall not eat it, nor shall you touch it, lest you die'" (Gen 3:2).

The serpent, Satan, taunted the woman, saying, "Surely you will not die! For God knows that in the day you eat of it your eyes will be opened and you will be like God, knowing good and evil" (Gen. 3:5).

Eve had been wandering in the garden and often wondered about that beautiful tree. It was exquisite, and she knew it was very special. As she walked close to it looking for food for the evening meal Eve looked at the tree thinking, "The serpent is probably right. My Lord wouldn't kill me and I won't die, He loves me too much. "Besides, I would love to be wise and know good from evil." With that she pulled the fruit from the tree and took it to Adam where they enjoyed the delicious fruit.

Suddenly, their eyes were opened and they both realized that they were naked, for up to this time they wore no clothes. Now, they were embarrassed and sought leaves big enough to cover themselves up.

As was the custom, God came into the garden that evening to walk with His human creations. Adam and Eve heard God walking in the garden, and they hid themselves from Him. The Lord called out to Adam, "Where are you?" But He already knew, for God is omniscient, all-knowing.

Adam slowly stood up with his head hung and said, "I heard Your voice in the garden and I was afraid because I was naked; and I hid myself."

> **Fear**
> *A feeling of dread or terribleness; frightened*

Fear is the first negative emotion recorded. All emotion up to that point was joy, peace, and a sense of well-being. Satan had assaulted mankind with his strongest tool; fear. Thus the first indication of evil was revealed in the garden as a result of disobedience. Fear continues to be a masterful tool over humans to keep them from achieving that which God has designed for mankind.

God, seeing the leaves covering His children asked, "Who told you that you were naked? Have you eaten from the tree of which I commanded that you should not eat?"

Adam defended himself, saying, "The woman that you gave to be with me, she gave me the fruit and I ate it."

God turned to Eve, and said, "What is this you have done?"

Then Eve cried, "The serpent deceived me and I ate." (Genesis 3:11-13)

God was angry, disappointed, and sad all at once. He was angry at Lucifer, the fallen angel, for having deceived Eve and then Adam. He was disappointed that they were so easily deceived, not remembering His command. And finally, the Lord God was sad because they had disobeyed Him and were now sinful. Their sin was disobedience, and their sin of disobedience came from rebellion. Now they would have to suffer the consequences; no one can disobey God without consequences. And the consequences were severe.

> **Rebellion**
> *To be bitter, change, be disobedient, disobey, to be grievous*

God had said if Adam and Eve ate of the Tree of the Knowledge of Good and Evil, they would die. Satan was partially right, which is his way of deception. He uses partial truth but twists it to where it is totally wrong.

In this case, Adam and Eve did not die a physical death. They lived many more years, but did eventually die a physical death. However, God had created the body of men to live forever. God created mankind to never be sick or know a moment of distress or torment. He had also created mankind to walk and talk with Him face to face. Now all that would change, simply because they didn't trust the word of their God.

Because of their rebellion, Adam, Eve and all their descendants, who include you and me, would be separated from God. No longer can we walk and talk with Him in face to face conversations. This was the ultimate death, for God withdrew Himself from the earth, never again to commune with mankind in the intimacy Adam and Eve knew.

Out of ignorance and being totally deceived, Adam and Eve delivered the dominion of the earth that God had given them, to Satan. The sinful act of eating the fruit from the forbidden tree had given Satan the legal right to take dominion over the earth. The keys of the kingdom had been transferred to the one who hated mankind. Satan is now in possession of the control of the earth and he subdues it with his divisive strategies.

Gleefully, Satan received that dominion. He now had the legal right to spew his vile intentions on the earth. Satan, the ultimate evil, could bring sickness and dis-ease to mankind. He could cause early deaths and give people tormenting thoughts that would drive them insane.

Satan would make life on earth a miserable existence in spite of the superiority and original dominion man had been given. They may succeed in business, but their personal lives will be shattered. Their personal life may be delightful, but their business will be embroiled in disillusionment. They may have money in the bank, but be bound with fear and anxiety. On and on were the plans of the dominion-bearer, Satan. Life on earth would become difficult and full of trials and tribulations because Satan now rules.

CHAPTER 4

The Kingdom Re-Enters the Earth

"Son, it's time." The Son looked up at the King and smiled a knowing smile. It *was* time! It was time to expand the Kingdom to a new region. "We must take back the dominion of Our Kingdom on earth that was lost to Satan," said the King, "I know the people are looking for a Savior because of the oppression they are under. They are crying out for someone to save them."

"But," the King continued to instruct, "You must go under cover. There will be no showy entry. No mass attacks by armies. This will be a 'covert' operation. We will take from within and the enemy won't know what hit him."

"I totally agree," said the Son. "The prophet has written that I am to be an 'unremarkable' person and one who will not stand out. I am ready, Father. To do it in this fashion, it will take more time than if an army were to attack," the Prince commented.

"Yes, but when You go," reminded the King, "You will have all my authority to back You. You will have my servants at Your beck and call. There will be hard times, but You will come out the victor." The Son replied, "I understand that, Father and I'm ready to do what must be done to restore peace and freedom in Our oppressed world."

"Son," said the Lord of Creation, "You will go to the earth and look as any other human. You will experience what they experience. You will have the feelings and emotions of a human. But, most of all, You are going to enter the territory of Satan because there is no human being that can do what You must do. You are the only one on the earth that will be able to redeem the sins of men and women. My law cannot be changed that says, 'Without the shedding of innocent blood, there is no remission of sins'" (Leviticus 17:11, Hebrews 9:22).

"It will be through Your sacrificial blood that will make humans, who are born into sin, pure enough for Me to once again have a relationship with My precious people."

"Go now," commanded the King "and I will be with You in Spirit."

"Father, I understand what I am to do," said the Prince, "I will become a human servant to show Your desires, Your love and power to them. I'll tell them of this Kingdom and what they can expect when We become victorious."

The King agreed saying, "The same government that is with Us here in Heaven, will arise in the earth once We have been victorious over Our enemy, Satan."

With that, the Prince left the total peace and joy of Heaven and entered a whole new world that was filled with hate, lust, greed and anger. "How sad," thought the Prince of Peace, "that there is so much misery in this world when it was meant to be full of peace, joy and love."

* * * * * * * * * * * * * * *

*For unto us a Child is born, unto us a Son is given;
and the government will be upon His shoulder.* Isaiah 9:6

* * * * * * * * * * * * * * *

CHAPTER 5

Thy Kingdom Come

To follow the orders of the King, the Prince entered the new world like any other mortal human being. He was born of a woman, but not any woman. She was a virgin, a sweet, gentle woman who loved God. When she was visited by an extraordinary being, the angel Gabriel, she was told that she was chosen above all others. The angel told her she would bear a son, the Son of God.

Of course she had a hard time imagining having a baby; after all she was only betrothed to Joseph. They weren't married yet. When she mentioned this to the angel, he said, "The Holy Spirit will come upon you and the power of the Highest will overshadow you; therefore, also, that Holy One who is to be born will be called the Son of God." (Luke 1:35)

At that point, she realized that there would be no physical contact with any mortal man, but be impregnated by a supernatural contact. She was overwhelmed with emotion, but managed to speak again to the angel, "Behold the maid-servant of the Lord! Let it be to me according to your word." (Luke 1:38)

The baby's DNA was not like other humans because His Father was extraordinary . . . supernatural. His Father was the King of all kings and Lord of all lords. He was . . . God. Now, God or Jehovah is a supernatural being. He has no flesh, but is a Spirit. He has always been and always will be. He is the Ruler of the Universe and the Most High God, El Elyon. No one has dared challenge God and succeeded. There had been one attempt, but it ended in disaster.

Lucifer made his futile take-over attempt and lost in the Kingdom of Heaven, but on the earth, he was the victor. He was able to intimidate, confuse and trick the woman in the Garden of Eden. Through the disobedience of Adam and Eve, the dominion of the earth was transferred to Satan. Now he held the keys of dominion and has played havoc through his simple methods of spreading fear, lust, pride, and rebellion. He didn't have to be very creative because man fell into sin easily.

In addition, all mankind are born a sinner simply because they are from the loins of Adam. So, for centuries Satan ruled and held dominion on the earth. Sickness reigned; corruption of man's bodies and minds was Satan's doing. Hatred, greed, violence, slander and lust all were birthed by the evil one of the earth, Satan. But things were going to change, for the Sin-bearer had come to earth.

Although born as a tiny infant, within that infant held the future of the world. The angels knew it, the animals of the field and the trees of the forest knew it. Only mankind, who had been corrupted by the enemy of our souls, did not realize it.

Only a few humans understood who this baby was. His mother, Mary, who had a visitation from the arch-angel, understood who the Christ child was. She had not been intimate with a human man, but was overshadowed by the Spirit of God and conceived this child. She knew his birth was miraculous.

Joseph, the man betrothed to Mary had every right to have her stoned because she was pregnant before their marriage. As he was contemplating what to do with his beloved, Joseph had a very vivid dream that he was to marry the pregnant Mary. Willing to take the humiliation and rejection of his family and friends, Joseph remained true to her.

Perhaps not known to Joseph, but the blood type of a child will always be the same blood type of their father. Since Joseph was not the father of this child in Mary's womb, the child did not carry normal, human blood. It was the blood of God, the Father, which flowed in the veins of the child soon to be known to the world as Jesus. The blood and DNA of God Almighty made Jesus all God and all human at the same time.

Joseph understood that the child in her womb was the Son of God and would save the world from their sins. But he had his doubts as the guardian father of this child. How could he, a poor carpenter, take care of this very special baby?

Elizabeth, Mary's cousin, knew the baby in Mary's womb was God's child when the child she was carrying leapt within her when they met. Upon their greeting each other, Elizabeth spoke with a loud voice and said, "Blessed are you among women and blessed is the fruit of your womb! But why is this granted to me, that the mother of my Lord should come to me? For indeed, as soon as the voice of your greeting sounded in my ears, the babe leaped in my womb for joy. Blessed is she who believed for there will be a fulfillment of those things which were told her from the Lord." (Luke 1:42-45)

CHAPTER 6

The Decree

Everyone in the village of Nazareth lived a normal life. Daily chores had to be done and there were birth and wedding celebrations. Work was an everyday task. Nobody rested but the very elderly and the small children. One day, a royal messenger came into the small village. There was a proclamation read commanding everyone to return to the village of their birth. Caesar Augustus, the governor, was commanding a census to be taken. Joseph, and the very pregnant Mary, had to go to Judea, to the city of David called Bethlehem where Joseph was born.

The trip through the dry, barren landscape was very hard. Mary rode upon a donkey or walked, but in her pregnant state, nothing was comfortable. Upon arrival, Joseph was desperate to find a place to rest because Mary was in labor. There were

The Decree

thousands of people in the village responding to the command so there were no rooms available.

Joseph was in a panic because the labor pains were coming strong and regular. He was determined not to let Mary deliver that very special babe in the street. Finally, God directed them to an inn where, although there were no rooms, there was a clean stable in the back.

So the baby was born with very little notice. This baby who was a Prince in Heaven has entered the earth as a King to bring the government of the heavenly kingdom to the earth.

A few shepherds in the field were startled on that special night when an announcement by an angelic host proclaimed the arrival of this King. They were told where to find the child who was born in the lowliest of places.

> **Redeemer**
> *One who buys back property, avenge, deliver*

Who would think that a king would be born in a stable filled with animals? Who would think the Redeemer of the world would lie in a manger in swaddling clothes? Yes, the King was born in humble means to prove a point. He came as a servant. He was noble in birth, but came in the

Mystery of the Kingdom of Heaven

lowliest of positions. This was a paradox that confused the spirit-world; to keep Satan off balance.

Although Jesus grew as a normal child, no one knew that He carried the Government of Heaven within him. Even Jesus himself did not consider himself anything other than a child that lived with a loving family. He showed no signs of importance. He was a wonderful child, who grew to a pre-teen, teenager, then young adult. He worked with His father, Joseph, in the wood shop as a carpenter. He loved everyone and helped those in need.

And, as a normal Jew, Jesus memorized the Torah and experienced His Bar-Mitzvah. He became a student of the Law of Moses and everything that had been written up to that point. In all His studies, Jesus loved to dig out its truths. He experienced life as a normal person, and even experienced the grief of losing His father to death.

As Jesus approached His thirtieth year, a new awareness was dawning in His mind. He began to realize that God was calling Him to be His spokesperson, His ambassador. There seemed to be a veil in Jesus' mind that was thinning between His natural, earthly existence and something incredibly bright and exciting. As Jesus

The Decree

contemplated what was dawning within Him, He reasoned it must be wonderfully supernatural.

As Jesus' days were filled with everyday life and work, He felt He had another mission on the earth. In God's perfect timing, Jesus knew within Himself that there was a destiny that He was called for, and it wasn't staying in Nazareth as a carpenter. He had been struggling within Himself as normal family life called him one way, but something within Jesus called Him to bigger and greater things. There was an ache in His soul that was crying out to be released. At that time, Jesus didn't know what that ache was, but before long He would know and be launched into a totally different life.

> **Destiny**
> *A pre-determined course of events that is established by a power outside of human existence*

The time had come to begin His earthly ministry; to begin spreading the good news of the Kingdom of God. Jesus' mind kept churning with thoughts that were coming from His Father in Heaven which He couldn't put into coherent thoughts. But one thing Jesus did know, He must strike out on His own to find that purpose that was nagging Him.

Mystery of the Kingdom of Heaven

One day, He approached His mother, Mary. "Mother," Jesus said, "it is time that I leave you and my family to be about my Father's business."

That one statement sent Mary's memory back in time. Jesus was only twelve years old when the family made their annual journey to Jerusalem for the Feast of the Passover.

When they had finished the days of celebration, they journeyed back to Nazareth with a large group of family members. Not knowing that Jesus lingered behind in Jerusalem, Joseph and Mary thought He was with other relatives in the group. After they went a day's journey, Mary and Joseph missed Jesus, and started looking for Him among the group. When they did not find Him, they returned to Jerusalem, seeking Him.

By this time, Jesus' parents were frantic because it had been three days since they left Jerusalem. Finally, they found Him in the temple, sitting in the midst of the teachers, both listening to them and asking them questions. And all who heard Him were astonished at His understanding and answers. So when His parents saw Him, they were amazed; and His mother said to Him, "Son, why have You done this to us? Look, Your father and I have sought You anxiously."

The Decree

And He said to them, "Why did you seek Me? Did you not know that I must be about My Father's business?" But they did not understand the statement which He spoke to them. (Luke 2:41-50)

As Mary pulled herself back to the present, she looked at her grown Son. She knew this time would come, but she didn't want to hear it. She said, "Jesus, You have been a wonderful Son and I have been honored to be Your mother. I know You are not really mine, but have always been God's."

She continued, "When kings from countries in other lands came bearing gifts, I knew that You would not always be with me." Choking back a sob, she whispered, "I knew that You would have to leave one day." She continued, "When you were just a young child, kings from the Far East came to worship and honor You. There were many treasures they gave as they worshiped You. Your father and I have kept them away in secret until now. What we have kept for You will cover all Your expenses as You go about your mission."

Tears spilled down her cheeks as she hugged her son goodbye. Mary said, "I will continue to pray that God will protect and guide You. Never forget, I love You with all my heart."

Jesus gave her one final hug and looked deep into her eyes. "You are truly a remarkable woman and I have been proud to call you My mother." Before the tears ran down his cheeks, he turned and went out the gate to begin what would be the end.

CHAPTER 7

Jesus Meets Cousin John

Jesus had heard that His cousin, John, was preaching along the river Jordan and felt an urgency to seek him out. John's mother, Elizabeth and his mother, Mary were cousins. It was Elizabeth who knew that Mary was going to bear the Son of God. The baby in Elizabeth's womb that leapt when Mary visited was the John whom Jesus was now searching for.

Although it would be a long journey, Jesus started walking over twenty-five miles from Nazareth to the northern part of Galilee. He was determined to find John because something within told Him it would be this visit that would launch Him into his future.

As He approached the river, it seemed everyone knew of the preacher called, John the Baptist. This

Jesus Meets Cousin John

"baptizer" was telling anyone who would listen that they were sinners and needed to repent. He kept saying, "Repent, for the Kingdom of Heaven is at hand." Then after they asked God to forgive them of their sins, he would baptize them in the river. That is why he stayed near the river banks.

> **Repent**
> To think; repentance is a decision that results in a change of mind, which in turn leads to a change of purpose and action

It was on one of these days that Jesus strode up to where John was preaching. There were many people; young and old, rich and poor, healthy and sick that were listening to what John was saying. He was bold and even looked a bit odd as he was dressed in camel's hair with a leather belt around his waist. But regardless, people understood that they were sinners needing forgiveness from God and were asking John to baptize them.

On this day, Jesus gently pressed through the crowd and approached John. He looked up, and seeing his cousin Jesus, immediately went to embrace him. Apparently John had been talking about someone who would be coming, and that he was just preparing the way for that Anointed One. At that moment, John and Jesus knew that this was the fulfillment of the prophetic words in Isaiah which said, *"The voice of one crying in the wilderness: Prepare the way of the Lord; Make His paths straight"* (Isaiah 40:3). The veil in Jesus' mind was fading quickly. He knew He was on the right road to his destiny.

Jesus asked John to baptize Him as he had done with all the other sinners. John was shocked, knowing that Jesus was sent by the Holy God of Israel. "Surely He is pure and clean already," thought John. "Why should I baptize Him?" Again Jesus asked John, "Please baptize Me." This time John spoke, "I need to be baptized by You, and here You are coming to me to be baptized?" (Matt. 3:14).

> **Water Baptism**
> *An act of obedience and a way to share with everyone that you are now committed to God and let Him be the center of your life*

Jesus answered and said to him, "Permit it just now, for this is the fitting way for both of us to fulfill all that is right" (Matt. 3:15). So John yielded and with utmost humility, baptized Jesus in the River Jordan.

When Jesus came up out of the water, the heavens above them opened and John saw the Spirit of God descend upon Jesus as light as a dove. Then a voice, strong and bold, came from the open heaven and said, "This is My beloved Son, in whom I am well pleased" (Matt 3:17).

Both Jesus and John understood immediately what had happened. Just as Isaiah had written so many years ago, Jesus is the one in whom the world had been waiting. Jesus, although a man, was also God; God in skin, the incarnate. Isaiah had written that He would be known as Wonderful, Counselor, Mighty God, Everlasting Father and Prince of Peace (Isaiah 9:6).

As these thoughts swirled in Jesus' human mind, He also felt an incredible power that was filling Him from head to toe. There seemed to be a Presence within Him that gave Him confidence, understanding, assurance and most of all, comfort.

Jesus stayed with John and enjoyed a meal and lots of laughter over their boyhood exploits. But throughout the visit, Jesus knew that something was growing stronger and stronger within Him. He knew that He must go into the wilderness on the other side of the river, alone.

In the morning Jesus said His goodbyes to John and his disciples. They prayed for each other as

Mystery of the Kingdom of Heaven

they shared a common urgency in telling others about what had just happened. With their final goodbye, Jesus crossed the river and walked into the stark landscape of the Judean wilderness.

He had no food, no bedding, and no water. He felt He just had to go into this direction. Although He didn't understand until days later that it was the Holy Spirit directing him, Jesus felt that a supernatural companion had compelled Him to approach this desolate land. It would be in this place that Jesus would meet all the supernatural players on this earth; Satan, God and their angels.

For days and weeks, Jesus communed with God through the Holy Spirit. It was in this environment of quiet solitude that Jesus learned His total purpose, the strategy He would take, and also the conflict that would arise as a result of His message. His message: the Kingdom of God would now be available to all who would accept Him as their Savior and receive His forgiveness and love.

> **Holy Spirit**
> *One of the Trinity having the responsibility to convict, communicate with sinners; to empower, teach and comfort those who are in the Kingdom of God*

Jesus would be the door or the path into the Kingdom. He would be the only way that mankind would find that intimate relationship with God that was lost in the Garden of Eden centuries before. Jesus would be the One who would show how much God loved them through teaching, preaching and healing those who would listen and believe. Then, when the time was right, Jesus would become the ultimate sacrifice by shedding His own innocent blood. This would satisfy God's requirement and redeem mankind back to Him.

It was during this time that Jesus realized that although He was all human, He understood that He was all God. He had been born of a virgin, grew up as a normal child, but having the pure, holy blood of God, was empowered by God through the baptism of the Holy Spirit. When He was baptized by John, it wasn't the water that erased the veil of understanding, but it was the baptism of the Holy Spirit. Jesus understood the water didn't make the change in His destiny, but His obedience to that urgent call that came from the voice within him, the Holy Spirit. And now, His journey would begin. The reason He left His beautiful Heaven to come to the earth and to mankind was to destroy the works that Satan had done to corrupt the peace, joy, health and wholeness that was lost in the Garden of Eden. (1 John 3:8)

CHAPTER 8

Jesus Meets Satan

Satan; the enemy of God and all mankind. When God expelled him from heaven, he became a totally different creature. He was no longer the most beautiful angel. He no longer carried the peace of Heaven within him or a song in his heart. Instead, he was filled with rage, hate and ready to get back at God through His own creation, mankind. While on earth, he was free to do his evil work and that was to kill, steal and destroy anything and everything that belonged to man. (John 10:10)

Satan knew that Jesus was a threat to his domain and could possibly end his reign of vile assaults on people. It was in this time, while Jesus was alone in the wilderness and physically weak that Satan decided to tease Jesus. His purpose was to tempt Jesus to set aside all his kingly authority and power and to prey on the weakness of Jesus' humanity.

Jesus Meets Satan

While sitting under a scraggly tree, Jesus' lips were parched from lack of water; he had lost weight and was weak from the lack of food for forty days. He had suffered from the heat of the sun during the day and the cold in the nights. But in the past five weeks, Jesus' constant companion was the Holy Spirit. In that desolate place Jesus communed with God and was reminded of the many things of the Kingdom that He would need to teach the people of the fathers of their ancestors. There was so much good news to share with God's precious people. Life was going to be so different if they would believe what He had to share with them. Jesus would not have traded his time with His Father for anything, so much so he was willing to neglect his own body.

As He reminisced what His Father had been telling Him, He heard a noise nearby. Opening His swollen eyes Jesus saw a form, but couldn't make it out. Then He heard the familiar voice of the fallen angel, Lucifer. "I've been waiting for you, Son of God," he hissed. "You may be strong in Heaven, but You are weak here in my dominion."

Knowing Jesus had been without food for nearly forty days, Satan commanded, "If You are the Son of God, command that these stones become bread" (Matt. 4:3).

Jesus, in a weakened voice lifted His head and said, "It is written, 'Man shall not live by bread alone, but by every word that proceeds from the mouth of God'" (Matthew 4:4).

Satan was not content to leave Jesus at that rebuff, so he tried a new strategy. Suddenly in a whirlwind, Satan took Jesus up into the holy city, set him on the pinnacle of the temple and said to Him, "If You are the Son of God, throw Yourself down. For it is written; 'He shall give His angels charge over you,' and 'In their hands they shall bear you up, lest you dash your foot against a stone" (Matt. 4:5-6).

Jesus knew Satan was trying to get Him to fall into the same trap he had set for Adam and Eve. Strength had returned to Jesus as He experienced this supernatural visit to Jerusalem with Satan. Yes, He was the Son of God, but He would not tempt God and His angels to protect Him so Jesus replied with great passion, "It is written again, 'You shall not tempt the Lord your God'" (Matthew 4: 7).

Before Jesus could blink an eye, He found Himself standing on a very high mountain. Satan waved his hand over the skyline and said to Jesus, "All these things I will give You if You will fall down and worship me" (Matt. 4:8-9).

Jesus was filled with great emotion. His first reaction was to laugh at the audacious request for Him to bow down and worship the one who was so corrupt he couldn't see his mistakes and worst of all, his future. The second reaction was one of reason. Satan wasn't out of line by saying he had the power to give the kingdoms of the earth to Jesus. Legally, he had every right to offer this to Jesus because Adam had released his dominion to Satan when he rebelled in the Garden of Eden. The keys of the Kingdom were still in Satan's possession.

As the Son of God, Jesus was going to take back what Adam released to Satan. But that was in the future and Jesus knew there was a lot to do before He would regain the dominion from Satan. Until then all Jesus wanted to do was get away from the presence of this evil. He burst with anger and cried out, "Away with you, Satan! For it is written, you shall worship the Lord your God, and Him only you shall serve" (Matt. 4:10).

With that, Jesus suddenly found Himself back under the scraggly tree in the wilderness, His incredible vision dissipated. He lay there only a few minutes when, once again, He heard a stirring nearby. When He opened His eyes, He saw beautiful, ethereal angels. In their arms, they carried water, fruit, bread and fresh clothes. They had been sent by His Father in Heaven to refresh and restore His mortal body so He could begin to tell His family, friends and the whole nation of Israel the good news that God had shared with Him.

> **Angels**
> *Heavenly attendants of God, functioning as messengers to make God's purpose known to men; they are also appointed by God to minister to believers*

His time in the wilderness was over and as He was renewed by the attending angels, He looked forward to His assignment to carry the message of the Kingdom to the people of Israel.

CHAPTER 9

Jesus Returns to His Hometown

Returning back to civilization, Jesus saw the people of His country with new eyes. He saw them with the eyes of His Father in Heaven. Those whom He knew as family, friends and His people of Israel were spiritually void of hope. They had been blinded in understanding how much God loved

> **Prosperous**
> *To push forward until one breaks out of circumstances; To move ahead advancing with victory in all areas of life*

them, and most of all did not comprehend the purpose each individual had while on this earth. God meant for them to rise above their circumstances, a destiny of victory in their personal, business, and physical life. God wanted all people to be prosperous. Jesus understood that only He, as the Son of God, could make this change in the environment upon the whole earth. Even though He saw the desperation in the hearts of God's children, He was excited to know that in the near future they would be able to make a complete change in their situations – if they only believed.

In Jesus' first visit to the synagogue upon His return to Nazareth from the wilderness, the priest gave Him the opportunity to speak. The book of Isaiah was handed to Him. When He had opened the book, He found the place where it read, *"The Spirit of the Lord is upon Me because He has anointed Me to preach the gospel to the poor; He has sent Me to heal the brokenhearted, to proclaim liberty to the captives and recovery of sight to the blind, to set at liberty those who are oppressed; and to proclaim the acceptable year of the Lord."* Then Jesus closed the scroll and gave it back to the attendant and sat down. All the eyes of everyone who were in the synagogue were watching Him. And He simply said to them, "Today this Scripture is fulfilled in your hearing" (Luke 4:16-21)

Many marveled at what Jesus had to say and others questioned saying, "Isn't this Joseph's son?" They were looking at Jesus as simply the carpenter's son and His human-ness. Jesus then responded to their unbelief by prophesying that once people in His hometown hear of the reports coming back from His missionary journeys, they will want the same done in their community. But Jesus said, "Listen, I say to you, no prophet is accepted in his own country." He knew that even though they will hear of His great exploits, they would still look at His humanity and not believe He is the Son of God. They will reason that Mary is His mother and Joseph is His father and they saw Him grow up as a little boy into manhood. Their memories would not allow them to accept the message He was bringing to the world. (Luke 4:22-24)

He continued to explain that in Elijah's ministry although there were many widows living in Israel during the famine, God sent Elijah to a Gentile woman to feed her. Again Jesus sited an example that in the time of Elisha there were many lepers, but God only cleansed a Gentile man named Naaman of Syria. When those sitting in the synagogue heard this, they got very angry and rose up, grabbed Jesus and led Him to the cliff of a hill so they could throw Him over to kill Him. But Jesus' angels cloaked Him and He walked right through the middle of the angry crowd and departed from His hometown. (Luke 4:25-30)

CHAPTER 10

Jesus Ministers to the Hopeless

For the next months and years, Jesus went about to all the villages and cities preaching the Good News of the Kingdom of God. This Kingdom that He had brought back to the earth was one of love, peace, health and joy. The Kingdom of God can dwell in everyone and Jesus wanted everyone to know that the Kingdom was available to them.

Everywhere He went Jesus saw the hunger for this Truth in the eyes of those who had been beaten down in life, felt defeated and were hopeless. He saw the demonic work of Satan starting to crumble when He commanded the unclean demonic spirits to leave the mortal humans as they were set free of oppression and depression. Jesus rejoiced with the lepers as their skin cleared up and was as fresh as a baby's skin. Time and again He touched the

Jesus Ministers to the Hopeless

blind eyes, the lame limbs, the deaf ears and the mute mouths and saw total restoration to their bodies. Minds were cleared from the blinders that Satan had put over the thoughts and reasoning of people. He had twisted the Truth just enough to pervert God's word that it caused confusion to pull mankind away from a victorious life. Jesus was delighted as He watched their right thinking restored. They once again had sound minds and were able to think intellectually. They knew what Jesus shared was true.

Thus, Jesus was fulfilling the prophesy in Isaiah that said, *"The Lord has anointed Me to preach good tidings to the poor; He has sent Me to heal the brokenhearted, to proclaim liberty to the captives and the opening of the prison to those who are bound; to proclaim the acceptable year of the Lord."* (Isaiah 61:1-2)

Many people started to relax, even in their present circumstances as they learned to trust God. They began to enjoy life and started laughing again. Entire communities were talking about Jesus and His message. Their thoughts began to be more hopeful as they looked to God for their provision, their healing and restoration. They

---
Trust
To have confidence; persuaded, an inward certainty
---

realized their answer was not their government, synagogue, family members or even themselves. They started believing that God was truly interested in their situations and that Jesus was delivering the answers that had been asked for generations. They started declaring that Jesus was the Messiah, believing that He was the Son of God.

CHAPTER 11

Jesus and His Disciples

When Jesus began His ministry, He knew His future was short. He needed men and women to learn the deep meanings and truths He was teaching. He knew that when He was gone, those that embraced His message and committed their lives to sharing His words and actions,

> **Disciple**
> *A learner or pupil that comes to a place of understanding what is taught and is convicted of the truth*

they would continue to spread the Good News. He called, as His inner circle, twelve common men from all walks of life. He didn't need kings, the military or religious priests. He wanted those who could relate and be accepted by the villagers and share this message quickly. As Jesus visited village after village, these men and women who supported

Jesus and His Disciples

Him in every way traveled with Him. They were His disciples.

These disciples lived with Jesus once He called them to join Him. They traveled with Him and heard all that Jesus taught day after day, month after month for over three years. They were able to gather all that Jesus was trying to convey for this new kind of life in the Kingdom of God. Even though the villagers heard only small portions or segments of Jesus' Good News message, His disciples got a deeper explanation and responded to whatever they heard. They received with what Jesus said was true. When they did, they were healed in their bodies and minds and were delivered from the hold that Satan had on them.

Faith

Such total assurance and confidence that one would act on that belief without evidence in the natural.

CHAPTER 12

The Blind Can See

It had been heard that Jesus and His disciples were in the town of Jericho. Jesus' reputation had preceded Him and the crowds were gathering. As they walked to the synagogue, a man who was blind and could only beg for a living began to cry out, "Jesus, Son of David, have mercy on me." He didn't think Jesus heard, so he cried out louder and louder, "Jesus, Son of David, have mercy on me." Not able to see, he just kept on yelling out trying to be heard above the crowd noises.

He was getting so loud, that many in the crowd wanted to quiet him. But Jesus *did* hear him and stopped walking. He told the disciples to bring the blind man to him. When they approached the blind beggar, they told him the Master wanted to see him. They said, "Be of good cheer. Rise, He is

The Blind Can See

calling you." With that, the man threw off his cloak that signified he was a beggar and went to Jesus.

Jesus had a question for the man who was obviously blind. "What do you want Me to do for you?" The man answered, "Rabbi, that I may receive my sight." Jesus was very impressed with this poor beggar. First of all the man recognized that Jesus was the Messiah by calling Him the Son of David. Secondly, he threw off a cloak that was a symbol of his plight of poverty and disability. When he did that, it showed Jesus that he had faith that he was going to be healed. When Jesus saw this man was convinced that Jesus could heal him, Jesus said, "Go your way; your faith has made you well." Immediately the man's sight was restored completely.

> **Faith Is Action**
> *When one is totally convinced of a truth, they will either speak or act on their belief.*

Leprosy was a skin disease that would create horrific nodules on the body and also deaden the nerve endings as well as cause paralysis. It made people hideous to look at and no one wanted a leper in their presence. It was a Law of Moses that those with leprosy had to stay away from family, friends and all of society. They were outcasts and lived in leper colonies where the sick would tend to each other. Family members would leave food at the outskirts of the colony, but never go in to visit.

It was out of these colonies that a certain man reasoned if Jesus could heal the blind, lame and deaf, then He could certainly heal a skin disease. When the man learned that Jesus was approaching his area, being filled with such desperation, he stood on an outcropping of rock just above the road and waited for Jesus and the disciples to walk by. When he saw the troupe approaching, it was then that he climbed down and stood on the road. As Jesus approached, the leper knelt down and said to Him, "If You are willing, You can make me clean."

Jesus knew the physical effort it took for him to make the trip as well as the risk of death, for it was forbidden for him to be out in public. Anyone could bring this to the attention of the priests and have him stoned. Pushing those thoughts aside, Jesus reached out and touched this man and with great compassion. "I am willing; be cleansed." (Mark 1:40-42) The disciples gasped when He physically touched the leper. At the same time Jesus was thinking, "Of course I am willing! I have come to set people like you free from this disgusting dis-ease that Satan has brought into the world. Of course I am willing that you live a life of productivity, love and laughter." At the love-response of Jesus' touch, the leprosy left our brave man and he was cleansed. Immediately everyone broke out in laughter and danced, rejoicing at what Jesus had done.

Thus, the disciples learned more to be Kingdom-minded and not rely on their religious traditions or experiences in their own life or family history. In place of a lifetime of training and living, they began to embrace the kind of mental renewal that Jesus was constantly teaching and demonstrating. In time, Jesus gave them authority over unclean spirits, to cast them out and to heal all kinds of sickness and all kinds of disease. One day, Jesus said, "You have heard Me enough, now I want you to go out two-by-two into the people of Israel. As you go, preach saying, 'the Kingdom of Heaven is at hand.' Heal the sick, cleanse the lepers, raise the dead and cast out demons. Freely you have received, freely give" (Matthew 10:1,6-8) .

The disciples were excited at the prospect of helping people. They did as they were commanded and saw amazing results, just as Jesus had promised. They returned all excited after a designated time, for each one of the disciples had stories to tell. They each glorified God for the opportunity to see the sick healed, the demon possessed delivered and the blind, deaf and maimed restored. These twelve men began to realize that they, too, had the supernatural power flow through them that Jesus exhibited. Jesus had given them permission to do what He did!

CHAPTER 13

Boy Delivered from Demonic Spirits

One day, Jesus came from the hills after being alone in prayer. As He approached His disciples, Jesus saw there were a lot of people surrounding them in great discussion. "What are you all talking about?" asked Jesus.

One of the men came out of the crowd and said, "Teacher, I brought You my son, who has a mute spirit. Whenever it grabs him, it throws him down; he foams at the mouth, gnashes his teeth and becomes rigid. I came for You, but You weren't here, so I asked the disciples to cast it out, but they couldn't."

Jesus looked at His friends and said, "You faithless people! How long must I be with you? How long must I put up with you?"

Boy Delivered from Demonic Spirits

You can understand His frustration when those same men had been out in the villages, casting out demons and healing the sick. They had experienced this same thing before, but now they could get no results.

Jesus said, "Bring the boy to me!"

But when the evil spirit saw Jesus, it threw the child into a violent convulsion and he fell to the ground, writhing and foaming at the mouth. "How long has this been happening?" Jesus asked the boy's father.

He replied, "Since he was a little boy. The spirit often throws him into the fire or into water trying to kill him. Have mercy on us and help us, if You can."

Jesus, possessing the attributes of God, knew exactly how long this child had been experiencing the demonic possession.

Constantly teaching, Jesus knew that if the disciples knew the length of time this child had been afflicted, they would see the significance of the miracle! Time isn't a factor in the matter of healing and demonic possession.

"What do you mean, 'If I can'?" Jesus asked. "Anything is possible if a person believes."

The father instantly cried out, "I do believe, but help me overcome my unbelief!"

When Jesus saw that the crowd of onlookers was growing, he rebuked the evil spirit. "Listen you spirit that makes this boy unable to hear and speak," He said. "I command you to come out of this child and never enter him again!"

Then the spirit screamed and threw the boy into another violent convulsion and left him. The boy appeared to be dead and a murmur ran through the crowd. "He's dead," remarked the people. But Jesus took him by the hand to help him to his feet and he stood up. (Mark 9:18-27)

The crowd was amazed and looked at Jesus with a new respect and began discussing among themselves believing that this truly must be the Son of God, the Messiah.

The disciples, still stung with the reality that they themselves couldn't help the boy asked Jesus, "Why couldn't we cast this demon out?"

Jesus replied, "This kind can come out by nothing but prayer and fasting." (Mark 9:28-29)

Boy Delivered from Demonic Spirits

The disciples then began to realize that they cannot expect the demonic world to respect their words unless they were in a close relationship with their Father in Heaven. Jesus had been an example of that by getting away by Himself to be with His Father in prayer each day.

Through Jesus' example, we must realize that if we want to be effective in the spirit realm, we must have a close relationship with God, the Father. It is His desire that we continually commune with Him to know His heart and mind so we may help others in their distress.

CHAPTER 14

You Must Be Born Again

Pharisee's were men who studied the Law of Moses written centuries before them. Their fathers and their father's father also studied the Law. Besides the original Law that God gave Moses, men had added more laws so difficult that they had to be explained. To study the Law and live by it became a life-long pursuit and their position in the synagogue was to explain the laws and make sure the Jewish people lived by them.

When Jesus started teaching and demonstrating the original intent of God's Law of love and honor, the Pharisees had a difficult time accepting what Jesus was saying. They were offended by the miracles that were taking place in His presence. Love was not part of their "Law." Simply obedience to these strict laws was required. So, there was a lot of discussion among the rulers of the synagogues and passions were rising.

One night a Pharisee, by the name of Nicodemus, sought Jesus out to speak to Him. He found Jesus by Himself and approached Him to ask questions. The questions were being asked by many in the synagogue and tempers were rising and Nicodemus wanted to get answers.

Jesus welcomed this distinguished visitor with grace. Nicodemus said to Him, "Rabbi, we know that You are a teacher who has come from God for no one can do these signs that You do unless God is with him."

Jesus gently answered and said to him, "Listen, I want you to know that unless one is born again, he cannot see the Kingdom of God."

Born again? Nicodemus couldn't comprehend how anyone could be born again! He loved God with all his heart and definitely wanted to see the Kingdom of God, but how could he possibly be "born" again? So, he asked Jesus, "How can a man be born when he is old? Can he enter his mother's womb a second time and be born?"

Jesus thought to Himself, "I have been waiting for someone from this sect to ask me the deep and important questions. I must be careful to explain this fully." So Jesus answered, "Listen to me carefully, unless one is born of water and the Spirit, he cannot enter the Kingdom of God. That which is born of the flesh is flesh, which is the natural birth. And that which is born of the Spirit is spirit."

Nicodemus was beginning to understand and nodded rubbing his beard.

Jesus continued, "Don't be amazed at what I am saying to you that you must be born again. The wind blows where it wishes, and you hear the sound of it, but cannot tell where it comes from and where it goes. So is everyone who is born of the Spirit."

Now Nicodemus was getting confused. This was getting complicated so he asked, "How can these things be?"

Jesus expected this response because Nicodemus was a man of religious teaching and only knew what he had been taught. But He came from the Kingdom of God in Heaven and knew the original intent of His Father.

You Must Be Born Again

Jesus answered saying, "Aren't you the teacher of Israel? Don't you know of these things?" "Listen to what I am saying, We (the Father and I) speak what We know and testify what We have seen and you don't receive Our witness. If I have told you about earthly things like the wind and you don't believe, how will you believe if I tell you heavenly things?"

Jesus continued, "No one has ascended to heaven but He who came down from heaven, which is the Son of Man, who is in heaven. And as Moses lifted up the serpent in the wilderness, even so must the Son of Man be lifted up. In that way, whoever believes in Him should not perish but have eternal life. For God so loved the world that He gave His only beloved Son that whoever believes in Him should not perish but have everlasting life."

"God did not send His Son into the world to condemn the world, but that the world, through Him, might be saved. He who believes in Him is not condemned; but he who does not believe is condemned already, because he has not believed in the name of the only begotten Son of God.

> **Condem, Condemnation**
> *To properly judge, conclude, punish, sentence*

This is the judgment, that the light has come into the world, and men loved darkness rather than light, because their deeds were evil. Anyone practicing evil hates the light and does not come to the light, lest his deeds should be exposed. But the one who does the truth comes to the light, that his deeds may be clearly seen, that they have performed and worked in God." (John 3:1-21)

> **Saved**
> *To deliver, protect, heal, preserve, do well, be made whole*

Although this was difficult to understand, as Jesus was talking, Nicodemus realized that this Man was the Messiah in whom the Jews had been waiting for so long. Here, in front of him was the Son of God, the Promised One.

What Nicodemus understood as Jesus was speaking was there is an action that must be taken in order to be a part of the Kingdom of God. To be born again, one must understand that God sent Jesus to the earth so that mankind could experience and know deep in their hearts that Jesus was the Son of God. By accepting Jesus, a supernatural transfer takes place and the Spirit of God will come into the one who believes. From that time on, that person is not condemned or punished by God, but is now His child and God becomes their Father.

Nicodemus' understanding was opened as he fell on his knees before Jesus. He spoke to Jesus with tears in his eyes saying, "I believe you, Jesus. I believe that you came from Heaven to share with us the love of God and His compassion on us here and now."

Jesus laid His hand on Nicodemus' head and blessed him. After a little more conversation, Nicodemus returned into the night with a greater understanding and appreciation for Jesus' ministry. Although he couldn't explain his emotions, Nicodemus felt as though a great weight had been removed from him. He felt joyful and wanted to dance and sing as he praised His God with much more emotion than he had ever done.

He knew the road would be difficult for both he and Jesus because of the conflict that Jesus was causing among his Rabbi friends. He also knew that with God on their side, both Jesus and he would accomplish what God had asked them to do.

CHAPTER 15

Don't Worry

As Jesus taught, He knew that people worried all the time. They worried about their families; they worried about their health, their livelihood; they worried about their past and they worried about their

> **Worry**
> *A distraction; a preoccupation with things causing anxiety, stress, and pressure*

future. Jesus knew that if the people would just accept His message and believed in their heart that God was in covenant with them that their worries would melt away. One day He gave a message to the people to help them understand.

He said, "Do not worry about your life, what you will eat or what you will drink; nor about your body, what you will put on. Is not life more than food and the body more than clothing?" Look at the birds of the air, for they neither sow nor reap nor gather into barns; yet your heavenly Father feeds them. Are you not of more value than they?"

Then Jesus went on to talk about clothing, that God dresses the beautiful flowers of the field, but thinks more of you, so don't worry about what you will wear.

Then He said something remarkable. Jesus said, "O you of little faith. Therefore do not worry saying, 'What shall we eat?' or 'What shall we drink?' or 'What shall we wear?' For after all these things the Gentiles seek. For your heavenly Father knows that you need all these things." Jesus was clearly explaining that worrying about our needs is a waste of time because God already knows what we need. If we are His children, then He will take care of us.

Jesus continued, "But seek first the Kingdom of God and His righteousness, and all these things will be added to you. Therefore do not worry about tomorrow, for tomorrow will worry about its own things. Sufficient for the day is its own trouble." (Matthew 6:25-34)

The important message that Jesus was trying to convey is that we are to earnestly look to God for our provision and to stay in a right relationship with Him. When we can do that, we will never have to worry about our needs.

This is probably the hardest message the disciples and those in attendance had to comprehend. They had always depended on parents, family members, the priests, and the government to take care of their needs. Now Jesus was telling them to look to God for EVERYTHING!

Through Jesus' gentle teaching, He was actually training the people to think covenant thoughts. They recalled that when God had made a covenant with Adam, Abraham, Isaac and Jacob He made a promise and never broke that promise. What Jesus was explaining to those

> **Covenant**
> *A binding agreement that cannot be broken by either party without penalty*

who would accept Him as the Messiah was that God, the Creator of the Universe was in covenant with them. He would provide for them, protect them, be a business partner, direct their lives and be totally devoted to them if only they would look to Him for all their needs in life.

CHAPTER 16

Jesus and the Parables

Jesus often spoke in parables. He would share what the Kingdom of Heaven is like. For example, one day, He was sharing a lot of parables about the Kingdom of Heaven. He said, "Again, the Kingdom of Heaven is like treasure hidden in a field, which a man found and hid; and for joy over it he goes and sells all that he has and buys that field." (Matthew 13:44)

> **Parable**
> *A fictitious story told to convey a message using common life illustrations but having spiritual application*

The disciples understood this to mean that the Kingdom of Heaven is so valuable that he would give up what he has in his natural life to accept what the Kingdom of Heaven has.

Another parable was understood when Jesus narrated, "Again, the Kingdom of Heaven is like a dragnet that was cast into the sea and gathered some of every kind, which, when it was full, they drew to shore. They sat down and gathered the good into vessels, but threw the bad away. So it will be at the end of the age. The angels will come forth, separate the wicked from among the just, and cast them into the furnace of fire. There will be wailing and gnashing of teeth." (Matthew 13:48-50)

Those listening looked at each other and easily understood this story. All people will be gathered at the end of days. Many are believers and will be kept close and live in the Kingdom of God. But those who are wicked and not believers will be cast into a terrible place with fire.

Sometimes even the disciples had a hard time comprehending this new way of thinking. The whole concept of the Kingdom of Heaven on earth was difficult. They had grown up thinking one way. Their fathers and their father's fathers had lived this way and now Jesus was asking them to consider this new way of thinking.

On one particular day, Jesus was speaking about dropping seeds in the soil. He said, "Behold, a sower went out to sow and as he sowed, some seed fell by the wayside; and the birds came and devoured them. Some fell on stony places, where they did not have much earth; and they immediately sprang up because they had no depth of earth. But when the sun was up, they were scorched, and because they had no root they withered away. And some fell among thorns and the thorns sprang up and choked them. But others fell on good ground and yielded a crop: some a hundredfold, some sixty, some thirty."

The disciples talked among themselves asking each other, "Did you understand the sower story?" It appeared that they didn't have a clear understanding, so they approached Jesus and asked, "What is the meaning of the parable of the sower?"

Before Jesus answered their question, He made a curious remark. He said, "To you it has been given to know the mystery of the Kingdom of God; but to those who are outside, all things come in parables so they can understand these stories better and repent of their sins." Then He said to them, "Do you not understand this parable? How then will you understand all the parables?" (Mark 4:10-13)

Patiently Jesus bent down and opened a bag of grain. As He pulled a handful of seeds out He then began to explain His parable. Dropping a few grains on the ground, He said, "The sower sows the word. And these are the ones by the wayside where the word is sown. When they hear, Satan comes immediately and takes away the word that was sown in their hearts." As He said this, Jesus swiftly took up the seeds to demonstrate Satan taking away the word.

Dropping a few more kernels a few inches apart from the first, Jesus continued, "These likewise are the ones sown on stony ground who, when they hear the word, immediately receive it with gladness; and they have no root in themselves and so endure only for a time. Afterward, when the tribulation or persecution arises for the word's sake, immediately they stumble."

Again, Jesus dropped seeds in another spot, "Now these are the ones," he said, "sown among thorns; they are the ones who hear the word and the cares of this world, the deceitfulness of riches and the desires for other things entering in choke the word, and it becomes unfruitful."

Taking the last seeds, Jesus sprinkled them saying, "But these are the ones sown on good ground, those who hear the word, accept it, and bear fruit:

some thirty-fold, some sixty and some a hundred." (Mark 4:14-20)

The disciples looked at each other in astonishment. How simple, they exclaimed to each other. They realized that not everyone would hear the word and keep it in their hearts. They also knew that Satan would try to steal or make every word questionable and people would begin to doubt this new way of thinking.

It was going to be more difficult than they thought. There was going to be much work to do in the future.

CHAPTER 17

A Few Loaves and Fish Feed Thousands

Jesus' popularity grew to where He had thousands waiting to hear what He had to say. They were constantly surrounded by people. One day Jesus and His disciples were attempting to find seclusion, away from the crowds, in the hills of Galilee. They all climbed in a fishing boat to cross the lake, but amazingly, the followers saw the boat that held Jesus and His friends. They followed it all the way around the large lake just to sit in His presence.

Jesus was so moved with compassion He docked the boat and went into the crowd to teach, forgetting His fatigue. He taught about the Kingdom of God and then healed the sick. As the day passed into late afternoon, a couple of His disciples asked Jesus to send the people away as it was very late and quite a distance to the nearest village that had food.

Jesus said something quite curious, He said, "They don't need to go away. You give them something to eat."

A little taken aback, the men dispersed to figure out how that could happen. After a little while, they came back to Jesus and said, "Rabbi, we have only five loaves and two fish from a child's lunch."

Jesus said, "Bring them here to me."

The disciples brought the little boy who held a basket with the bread and fish. Jesus looked at the child with such love, that the boy fell at His feet. Perhaps he had never experienced the feeling that someone really cared and appreciated him.

At Jesus' command, the disciples had everyone present sit down on the grass in small groups. Then Jesus took the five loaves and two fish, and looking up to heaven, He blessed and broke and gave the food to the disciples – all twelve of them. The disciples then gave to the multitudes. To their amazement, their baskets never emptied. Of the 5,000 men present, each ate until he was full. Similarly, all the women and children present ate till contented. This means well over 15,000 people ate from the five loaves and two fish.

When all were fully satisfied, the disciples passed the baskets to pick up what was left. To their amazement, each of the twelve baskets returned to them full of the same bread and fish! Truly, Jesus was demonstrating how God will provide when you trust Him. (Matthew13:13-21)

CHAPTER 18

Moved by Faith

One thing that always impressed Jesus was the faith of people who had a deep desire for a change in their lives or the lives of others. One memorable day, Jesus was walking through Capernaum when a small contingent of Jewish elders appealed to Him regarding a centurion whose beloved servant was sick and dying.

The Jews had been very impressed with this Greek military man saying that he was deserving of Jesus' attention by saying, "He loves our nation, and has built us a synagogue." They also explained how precious this servant was to the centurion. Jesus, who was convinced, started toward the centurion's home.

When He was only a short way from the house the centurion sent friends to Him saying, "Lord, do

Moved by Faith

not trouble Yourself, for I am not worthy that You should enter under my roof. Therefore I did not even think myself worthy to come to You. But say the word, and my servant will be healed. I am a man placed under authority, and having soldiers under me I understand that when I say to one, 'Go,' and he goes; and to another, 'Come,' and he comes; and to my servant, 'Do this,' and he does it."

Jesus was amazed at his logic and marveled. He then turned to the crowd that followed Him and said, "I say to you, I have not found such great faith, not even in Israel!" Then those who were sent went into the house of the centurion and found the servant well. (Luke 7:1-10)

Everywhere Jesus went, the people came, bringing to Him the lame, blind, mute, maimed, and many others. They would lay their friend or family member at Jesus' feet with great anticipation. Jesus never said to them, "You don't know enough," or, "I can't heal you." He never said, "No, I won't heal you." or "It is not My will to heal you." No, whoever came to Him believing that He could heal, He would heal them.

The multitudes would marvel when they saw those who hadn't spoken for years, speak. They shouted for joy when the maimed were made whole and the lame walked. They rejoiced when the blind finally saw colors and forms of people. With these signs and miracles, the people glorified the God of Israel. (Matthew 15:30,31)

When we step forward believing that Jesus can and will heal, with no doubt in our heart, that is faith. Faith is action and when we take action on His word, He will do as we ask.

One day to demonstrate this Law of God, Jesus and His disciples were hungry and looking for fruit on trees. They saw a fig tree and looked to see if there were figs on it. Although the tree had leaves, there were no figs, for they were not yet in season.

Jesus wanted to teach the disciples a lesson on how powerful words were, so He said to the tree, "Let no one eat fruit from you ever again."

The disciples looked at each other wondering what that was all about. The next morning, they walked by the same fig tree and saw the tree dried up from the roots. One of the disciples remembered that Jesus had cursed the tree said, "Rabbi, look! The fig tree which You cursed has withered away."

So Jesus answered and said to them, "Have faith in God. For assuredly, I say to you, whoever says to this mountain, 'Be removed and be cast into the sea,' and does not doubt in his heart, but believes that those things he says will be done, he will have whatever he says. Therefore, I say to you, whatever things you ask when you pray, believe that you receive them, and you will have them." (Mark 11:12-24)

One of the most important lessons Jesus taught and demonstrated over and over again was the power of words. We have the power of God within us through our belief in the life and sacrifice of Jesus Christ. When we speak words with authority and conviction that are in line with the word of God, then the Law in Mark 11 will apply to you.

CHAPTER 19

The Day of Great Miracles

Another time Jesus was on His way through a village to help a distressed father when it was reported that his daughter was on the verge of death. Jesus was on His way to the home of the child and, as usual, there was a crowd that followed Him. On this day there seemed to be more people than normal for they were pressing against His disciples and Himself. It seemed as if everyone just wanted to touch Him or get a glimpse of Him.

But in all of this jostling, suddenly Jesus felt power go out of Himself. He looked around trying to see what could have caused this and asked "Who touched My clothes?" The disciples looked at each other, then at the crowd. Pointing at the people, one of the disciples said, "You see these people

The Day of Great Miracles

all around You, and You want to know who touched You?"

Immediately, Jesus spotted a woman on her knees with tears in her eyes looking up at Him with a glowing countenance. He reached out to her and raised her up. She then told Him her story. She had been sick for over twelve years with an issue of blood. Although she had been to many doctors looking for a cure she still was not healed. In addition, her savings was completely gone.

The woman knew the risk she took by entering the throng of the people, because the Law of Moses said she would be stoned if caught. But she had heard of Jesus and felt that she would be healed even if she only touched the hem of His garment. She believed she could be healed!

She continued saying, "I just kept pressing through all these people and was knocked to the ground. I knew that if I just touched the hem of your robe, Rabbi, I would be healed. I pushed and finally stretch out to touch you and instantly I felt power course through my body." With that, tears of worship and thanksgiving flowed.

Jesus looked upon her and said, "Daughter, your faith has made you well. Go in peace and be healed of your affliction." (Mark 5:25-34)

Faith always touched Jesus. When people trusted that Jesus was the Healer sent by God, they saw immediate results. Lepers, the

> **Faith**
> *The highest form of belief; It is a conviction that causes one to take action through either speech or doing something.*

blind, fathers and mothers, men of other religious sects all began to believe in their heart that Jesus was truly the Messiah, the Sent One from God. When they did believe, immediately their blind eyes saw, legs were strengthened, fevers left. Even the dead came back to life through the faith of their loved ones.

Once Jesus and the disciples left the woman that was healed, they continued to the home of Jairus. He was a ruler in a synagogue who had a small daughter who was dying. He came asking for Jesus' help saying, "My little daughter lies at the point of death. Come and lay Your hands on her, that she may be healed, and she will live." Even as Jesus and His disciples were still making their way to the home, one of the servants came to the ruler and said, "Your daughter is dead. Why trouble the Teacher any further?"

> **Believe**
> *To trust in, have faith in or be totally persuaded, not only in the mind but in the heart*

When Jesus heard this message, He turned to the ruler of the synagogue and said, "Do not be afraid; only believe." The father, although quite distraught, believed that Jesus could help his daughter. Even though they said she was dead, Jesus continued walking to the house.

When they arrived, the paid mourners had already arrived and were wailing and crying in loud voices. Many family members were beginning to arrive joining in the wailing, making so much noise it was hard to hear any conversation.

Jesus turned to His disciples and asked that only He and three others, Peter, James and John accompany Him into the house. What He needed at this time, were men whose belief would not be swayed by what they saw. In the natural, death is final. But in the spiritual, depending on the depth of the believer's faith, the natural can be changed from impossible to very possible. So, the small group of men entered the house and found the father, who was the ruler of the synagogue and his wife holding on to each other for support as all the mourners that surrounded them were lamenting.

Jesus, seeing the disturbance by the mourners who were weeping and wailing, went up to them and asked, "Why make this commotion and weep? The child is not dead, but sleeping." They looked at Him and laughed, ridiculing Him. With that, Jesus had them all leave and He took the father and the mother of the child, as well as the disciples, with Him into the room where the child was lying.

With all those present who believed that Jesus would restore the child back to life, He took the child by the hand and said to her, "Little girl, I say to you, arise."

Immediately the child took a gasp of breath and began to breath, opened her eyes, and sat up. As the small group looked on in total amazement, she stood up. Although they knew Jesus could raise the dead, they were very surprised, when it actually happened. Jesus wasn't surprised, for He knew He was the Life that can heal the sick and raise the dead.

He was smiling with the understanding that people would talk about this for a long time. But in jest,

The Day of Great Miracles

He told those present not to tell anyone! Then in a loud voice Jesus declared, "Give this girl something to eat!" And they all laughed and celebrated the goodness of God. (Mark 5:35-43)

CHAPTER 20

The Religious System

If Jesus understood anything, it was the role Satan played in perverting the Truth. When God gave Moses the laws by which mankind was to live, it was simple and laid out so that man would be blessed by God.

> **Blessed**
> *A cause for celebration*

But when Satan got involved in the earth and corrupted man's reasoning, those laws were multiplied and became very cumbersome. It was his way to have power and control over mankind. Satan used the religious establishment to bind and subdue the freedom people were given. So when Jesus came to the earth, He saw so much perversion of the original Law that He was greatly disturbed. When the priests of the most powerful groups of Jews, the Sadducees and the Pharisees heard what

The Religious System

Jesus was preaching, they felt threatened and their hearts rebelled against His liberating messages.

Little things about Jesus really disturbed them. On one Sabbath, Jesus and His disciples were hungry. As they walked through a field of grain, they started snapping the heads off and popped it in their mouths. According to the "revised" Law of Moses these men were not to work on the Sabbath. The priests considered what they were doing as work and complained to Jesus.

Jesus responded with a story from the time of King David. He reminded them that King David, who was also a Jew, ate when he was in need and hungry. At that time, King David also went into the Temple and ate the sacred showbread which had been sanctified for the Lord. Jesus gave them insight by saying, "The Sabbath was made for man, and not man for the Sabbath. Therefore the Son of Man is also Lord of the Sabbath." (Mark 2:23-28)

What Jesus was saying was He was the Master of the sacred day of the week. He wrote the rules, but it seemed as though man and his need for power had become more important than observing the Sabbath.

To make this more clear, Jesus was attending the synagogue one Sabbath as was His custom. Even though He was God, He continued to observe the Sabbath as prescribed in the Torah. On this particular day there was a man attending who had a withered hand. He hid it in his clothes because it was appalling to see. Jesus knew this man was in need, so His attention was drawn to him. At the same time, the priests watched Jesus to see if He would heal on the Sabbath, which they considered work. They asked Jesus, "Is it lawful to heal on the Sabbath?"

Calling the man to Him, Jesus said, "Is it lawful on the Sabbath to do good or to do evil, to save life or to kill?"

"What man is there among you who has one sheep and if it falls into a pit on the Sabbath, will not lay hold of it and lift it out? Of how much more value then is a man than a sheep? Therefore it is lawful to do good on the Sabbath."

The priests said nothing. Their attitude made Jesus angry because they obviously didn't care about the man, but only wanted to keep a law that had been established by the perversion of God's simple Law. The way Jesus explained, the Pharisees had made it understood that helping someone in need on the Sabbath was work and therefore a sin! Jesus never wanted laws to override helping others. So, Jesus said to the man, "Stretch out your hand."

The Religious System

As the man stretched out his contorted hand, it was totally restored. It was this man's obedience that caused it to be healed. If the man kept his hand inside his garment, he would not have received his healing. But through his faith and action to Jesus' word, his hand was fully restored.

Amazingly, this angered the Pharisees so much that they started planning how to destroy Jesus' image, His influence and even His life. Because Jesus was challenging their authority and drawing people away from their religious thinking, they knew He was a threat to their way of life and their very careers. To them, the sacrifice one man for the sake of their religion was better than to lose influence and power over the people. (Matthew 12:9-14/Mark 3:1-6)

Jesus was quite aware of their conspiracy. He knew He was on the earth for one purpose and that was to restore the Kingdom of God back to the earth and return the dominion and authority of God back to man. Jesus was always focused on the end and determined to reach it. There was no one else, no mortal man, who could accomplish the destruction of the power and authority of Satan. Only Jesus.

CHAPTER 21

Power of Binding and Loosing

More than once Jesus taught about the authority believers would have over the tactics of Satan. The disciples had experienced great victories over Satan and his devices when they commanded sickness, fever, and many different kinds of unclean spirits known as demons to leave people. Jesus demonstrated this spiritual law one Sabbath when He was in the synagogue.

Jesus knew it was Satan who was responsible for the agony, suffering and distress in the world. On one particular Sabbath day, Jesus saw an old woman who was so bent over her nose touched her knees. She couldn't rise to stand up, but walked bent over. Jesus had compassion on her because she had a spirit of infirmity. He learned that she had been like that for eighteen years.

Power of Binding and Loosing

Jesus called her to Him and said, "Woman, you are loosed from your infirmity." He laid His hand on her and immediately she was made straight and praised God. Again, the ruler of the synagogue was indignant because Jesus had healed someone on the Sabbath. The man called out to the crowd and said, "There are six days on which men ought to work; therefore come and be healed on another day and not on the Sabbath day."

> **Loose, Loosed (verb)**
> *Loosen, break up, destroy, dissolve, melt, put off*

Jesus then answered him and said, "Hypocrite! Does not each one of you on the Sabbath loose his ox or donkey from the stall and lead it away to water it? So ought not this woman, being a daughter of Abraham, whom Satan has bound – think of it – for eighteen years, be loosed from this bond on the Sabbath?"

> **Bind, Bound**
> *To be in bonds, knit, tie, wind*

With that, Jesus' accusers hung their heads with shame while everyone else celebrated what God had done for their dear sister. (Luke 16:10-17)

Jesus had been teaching His disciples God's intended understanding of His love and laws. He had come to the earth from Heaven to deliver the message that they would soon have the power and authority over the enemy, Satan and his evil spirits.

On two occasions, Jesus instructed His disciples on this authority. The first, when He was discussing the power over the enemy with His disciples. He said, "I say to you that you are Peter, and on this rock I will build my church, and the gates of Hades shall not prevail against it. I will give you the keys of the Kingdom of Heaven, and whatever you bind on earth will be bound in Heaven, and whatever you loose on earth will be loosed in Heaven." (Matthew 17:19)

The keys of the Kingdom of Heaven mentioned were not physical keys, but they were a symbol of the power that Jesus would deliver in the future. These keys could be used once Jesus had fulfilled His assignment on earth. The power and authority He would make available to those who believed in Him would make it possible to bring the power of heaven to earth. If God, the Father, dis-allows something in heaven, it can be bound and dis-allowed on earth. If there is a situation that is perfectly acceptable in heaven, then it can be loosed on the earth.

Power of Binding and Loosing

Another time, Jesus was instructing His followers how to handle a fellow believer when he was disobeying (sinning against) God and fellow believers. Jesus knew that the "one" who motivates disobedience is Satan. Therefore, He explained the principle of binding and loosing once again by saying, "Assuredly, I say to you, whatever you bind on earth will be bound in Heaven, and whatever you loose on earth will be loosed in Heaven. Again I say to you that if two of you agree on earth concerning anything that they ask, it will be done for them by My Father in Heaven. For where two or three are gathered together in My name, I am there in the midst of them. (Matthew 18:18-20)

Binding the rebellious behavior of a person is done in the spirit realm because it is Satan who motivates a person to sin. Jesus knew that upon the fulfillment of His assignment on the earth, that mankind would be able to stop Satan's maneuvers when they understood their power and authority over Satan's maneuvers. By loosing Heaven's powers is releasing the angelic host to work on behalf of the believers. It takes the Army of Heaven to war against the Army of Satan. Jesus was revealing a new way to deal with the tactics of the enemy of man.

CHAPTER 22

Learning To Pray

As Jesus taught the people of the villages, He continued to teach deeper truths to His disciples. They were beginning to understand who Jesus was, why He was there, but still thought like their fathers in many ways. Yet, Jesus was beginning to stir revelation within them to the point where they were breaking free from tradition.

An example of breaking free from tradition was in the way they prayed. Jesus was a man of great prayer and taught His followers how to pray a prayer that would make a difference in their lives. He quickly taught them that those who prayed in the synagogues and on the streets were vain. They would stand beating on their chests saying how great they were and what they did for God. They were actually hoping to impress anyone who heard.

But Jesus explained, "Don't be like them. Go into a secret place and be His friend. Talk to Him like He's your Daddy. Jesus explained that our Father in Heaven knows what we need even before we ask Him. But what God the Father wants is for us to acknowledge Him as the One who can hear and respond to our prayers. (Matt 6)

Jesus then taught how to pray saying, "Our Father in Heaven, hallowed be Your name. This opening line reveres God as the One True Living God, the Only God, the Most High God, also known as El Elyon.

He went on to say, "Your kingdom come, Your will be done on earth as it is in Heaven." This was Jesus' way to say, we have the right to command what God has set in place in Heaven to be done here on earth. Jesus' whole purpose on earth was to bring the Kingdom of Heaven and the dominion that belongs to man back to the earth. With this statement, we are acknowledging that we understand what is in Heaven which is total peace, health, joy, adulation, worship, and contentment. Jesus knew this can be on the earth just as it is in Heaven.

"Give us this day our daily bread." Jesus continued to stress the importance of relying on God for daily provision and to trust Him for everything.

"And forgive us our debts as we forgive our debtors." (Matthew 6:9-15) Jesus knew this was a big hurdle for people to overcome. He explained, "If you forgive others the things they have done to you, then your heavenly Father will also forgive you. But if you don't forgive others the things that offended you, grieved you, hurt you or destroyed things in your life, then neither will your Father forgive the things you have done to offend, grieve, hurt or destroy others' lives. (Mark 11:25,26)

This model prayer that Jesus gave to His disciples to pray was just that, a model. It is like an outline or the bones by which we structure prayer. So as we learn to commune with our Father in Heaven we can think of it as doing business with Him. Recognize who God is. Know that He is your Provider. You have a right to acknowledge what is in Heaven can be done on earth.

We must also understand that forgiveness is essential in order to have God forgive us. If God cannot forgive us because we don't forgive others, then we cannot enter the Kingdom of Heaven because we are being rebellious against God's law. Forgiveness is also necessary for God to be able to hear our prayers.

CHAPTER 23

Understanding Who Jesus Is

Jesus was always a man of surprises. He never did things in a normal, conventional way. There was a time when He and His twelve disciples got into a boat to rest. While in the middle of the sea, a great storm arose. The waves were so high that the boat was in great peril. Many of the disciples were fishermen and used to storms, but this one was frightening them. They really thought the boat was going to capsize. In spite of the fact Jesus was sleeping soundly, they decided to wake Him up. They cried out to Him, "Lord, save us! We are perishing!"

When He woke up and realized what was happening, He said to them, "Why are you afraid? You of little faith?" Jesus was disappointed that they didn't have confidence that because He was in the boat that nothing would happen to them. Again, teaching them through action, Jesus stood up and rebuked the winds and the sea. Immediately the waves calmed and the winds ceased. The men in the boat marveled saying, "Who can this be, that even the winds and the sea obey Him?"

On another occasion, Jesus was discussing the purpose He came. "Do not think that I came to bring peace on earth," Jesus said. "I did not come to bring peace, but a sword. For I have come to set a man against his father, a daughter against her mother and a daughter-in-law against her mother-in-law; and a man's enemies will be those of his own household." He continued, "He who loves father or mother more than Me is not worthy of Me. And he who loves son or daughter more than Me is not worthy of Me. And he who does not take his cross and follow after Me is not worthy of Me. He who finds his life will lose it, and he who loses his life for My sake will find it." (Matthew 10:34-39)

In this difficult lesson, Jesus wanted to make it clear who people were embracing as Savior. They were declaring Him as Messiah, Son of God, however He wanted them to know that it was not going to be easy. Because as surely as one accepted Him as their Lord, those nearest to them would be against that decision. Satan will make sure that family members would come against them and even cast them out of their lives.

On the flip side, we must be careful not to make other people or things more important than our relationship with the Father. Part of making a covenant or binding agreement with God through the acceptance of Jesus being His Son, was the responsibility of not denying the fact that He is Lord and Master of your life. In many cases, this could be very difficult and would take a great deal of sacrifice and discipline. Our decisions now will determine how Jesus will represent us when we stand before God in Heaven.

However, Jesus also wanted those listening to know the positive side of being a follower of His by saying, "Whoever confesses Me before men, him I will also confess before My Father who is in Heaven. But whoever denies Me before men, him I will also deny before My Father who is in Heaven." (Matthew 10:32-33) It is important to realize that when we tell people He is part of our life; He is our Protector, Provider, Healer, Savior, then He will be able to tell His Father in Heaven all about you.

Many months later, Jesus was with His disciples and asked, "Who do men say that I, the Son of

Man, am?" Several of the disciples threw out the opinions of the people. Then Jesus said, "But who do you say that I am?" It was then that Simon Peter, the one who boldly spoke His mind, answered "You are the Christ, the Son of the living God."

Looking very pleased, Jesus answered and said to him, "Blessed are you, Simon Bar Jonah because flesh and blood has not revealed this to you, but My Father who is in Heaven." Of course, Peter was proud that he had understood the deity of Jesus, but what Jesus said next astounded not only Peter but all present.

Jesus continued to say, "I also say to you that you are Peter and on this rock I will build My church and the gates of Hell shall not prevail against it." This was the first time there was any mention of "church" which would not be established until after Jesus left the earth. The disciples were awestruck as Jesus continued to prophesy to them. "I will give you the keys of the Kingdom of Heaven and whatever you bind on earth will be bound in Heaven, and whatever you loose on earth will be loosed in Heaven." (Matthew 16:13-19)

> **Peter**
> *Rock, a smaller part of a much larger rock*

It would take the disciples a long time to unravel the elusive words of this profound statement. One thing they did understand was that they were given power right then and there to use words to command the things that are in Heaven to happen on earth when they spoke it. They also had the power to bind the works of the devil with commanding power. All this was delivered by Jesus through His words however the disciples didn't know what to do with His statements until much later.

CHAPTER 24

Jesus Is The Only Way

On several occasions Jesus delivered a message that showed people how to live forever with the God of Creation, the God of Love, the God of Restoration, His Father. Jesus knew that He was to bring the Kingdom of Heaven to the earth, but also knew that it is appointed for men to die in the flesh. God ordained men to live a certain number of years on this earth, but eventually their mortal bodies would stop functioning. The heart would stop pumping, the blood stop flowing, the brain stop functioning. At that moment man would be dead in his physical body.

Our body is flesh which is corruptible. That means it will decay when we die. But the moment we die, our souls, that is our mind, personalities and even emotions will continue on forever. We will be able to see, smell, feel emotions and react to what is around us. Regardless of what any people, religious, or non-religious people say, we will go into eternity with our thoughts and memories.

Heaven is a place that is eternal. It is a real place for our real souls. The place that a believer in Jesus Christ will spend eternity is a place of peace, joy, satisfaction and surrounded by love. Imagine being in a place of total security, peace and love forever. When a person who has believed that Jesus is the Son of God, breathes their last breath on this earth, they will continue to live forever with God in a place called Heaven.

Another place that is eternal is a place that is dark and terrifying. It is called hell or hades. Hell was made for the devil and his angels. God never meant for mankind to inhabit hell because it is total separation from God. When Adam and Eve rebelled in the Garden, their disobedience separated them from God and they became sin. Sin is not allowed in God's presence, so there is no way a sinner can live eternally in Heaven where God is.

That is why Jesus had to come to the earth. He was to be the ultimate sacrifice, by shedding His blood and take all our sins upon Himself so we could become sinless. Unless you believe and accept that Jesus is the Son of God and became the sacrifice to take away the sins of this world, you cannot enter Heaven. Those that make Jesus Lord of their lives will never have to experience a moment of hell.

Hell is literally such a dark place you can't see your hand in front of your face. Satan will rule hell which means it will be full of wicked, frightening creatures that are meant to torment the occupants. The worst thing about hell is that Jesus will never reside there. There will be no love, compassion or forgiveness. Without Jesus, it will be a hopeless, frightful, horrible place. When Jesus Christ came to the earth, He shared what hell is like. He doesn't want a single person to go there, but wants people to believe in His Word and spend all the days of eternity with Him.

Jesus shared this with His followers. He said, "Let not your heart be troubled; you believe in God, believe also in Me. In My Father's house are many mansions; if it were not so, I would have told you. I go to prepare a place for you. And if I go and prepare a place for you, I will come again and receive you to Myself; that where I am, there you may be also. And where I go you know, and the way you know." Thomas, one of the disciples

> **Receive**
> *Associate with oneself in a familiar or intimate act or relation*

asked, "Lord, we do not know where You are going and how can we know the way?" (John 14:1-5)

Jesus smiled and answered him and said, "I am the way, the truth and the life. No one comes to the Father except through Me." (John 14:6) Jesus said that because He knew there were many ideologies in the world that speak of different ways to be 'with God.' Jesus wanted them to know there was no other man, idol, chant, work or act by which they could reach eternity with God. He continued, "If you had known Me, you would have known My Father also, and from now on you know Him and have seen Him." (John 14:7) The disciples nudged each other knowing they had seen many miraculous events and signs that were done supernaturally.

Then Philip one of His disciples, asked Him, "Lord, show us the Father, then we'll be satisfied." Jesus said to him, "Have I been with you so long and yet you have not known Me, Philip? He who has seen Me has seen the Father; so how can you say, 'Show us the Father?' "Do you not believe that I am in the Father, and the Father in Me? The words that I speak to you I do not speak on My own authority; but the Father who dwells in Me does the works. Believe Me that I am in the Father and the Father in Me, or else believe Me for the sake of the works themselves." (John 14:8-11) With that, each disciple had their own memory of the amazing miracles they had seen Jesus perform. They remembered the love and extreme compassion Jesus had for everyone. However, Jesus knew that with the Holy Spirit that dwelled in Him would soon be in all those who believed.

Then Jesus said something that gave the disciples a thrill. He said, "Most assuredly I say to you, he who believes in Me, the works that I do he will do also; and greater works than these he will do, because I go to My Father. And whatever you ask in My name, that I will do, that the Father may be glorified in the Son. If you ask anything in My name, I will do it." (John 14:12-14) The disciples looked at each other amazed! If they heard right, Jesus was giving them the same power and authority that He carried when they believed in Him! They also understood that Jesus' name could be a key to victory over Satan.

> **Glorified**
> *Esteemed, Honor, Praise, Worship*

Jesus knew what would happen in the future. Looking at the people milling around Him in the market, Jesus knew these men and even women who had witnessed the miracles and heard His explanation of the Kingdom of Heaven had a great future ahead of them. Not only for those who stood with Him now, but in future years and generations to come. Those who could not only read of what had happened in the days of the original disciples, but those who would be born in the 1600's, 1700's, 1800's, 1900's and the 2000's would also receive the authority and power that Jesus held.

Jesus continued His musing. Those who would believe and receive Jesus' birth and life and future death not only in their minds, but in their hearts, would receive the indwelling of the Holy Spirit; the companion, teacher, and protector of their hearts. That indwelling is the same as having the Father God and Jesus the Christ within them spiritually.

On another day, Jesus had told the growing crowd around Him about Satan and what his job description involved. Jesus gave a

> **Saved**
> *Delivered, protected, healed, preserved, saved from self, be made whole, do well*

word picture of a shepherd and his sheep. He said, "Most assuredly I say to you, I am the door of the sheep. All who ever came before Me are thieves and robbers, but the sheep did not hear them. I am the door. If anyone enters by Me, he will be saved, and will go in and out and find pasture." "The thief (Satan) does not come except to steal, and to kill, and to destroy. I have come that they may have life, and that they may have it more abundantly." (John 10:10)

> **Abundantly**
> *Superabundance, excessive, overflowing, surplus, over and above, more than enough*

Jesus was giving His followers the insight of how the two spiritual entities work. Satan is dark, evil, wants to destroy, and keep anyone from moving ahead with success. Jesus, on the other hand, desires just the opposite. He is light, hope, joy, peace, and desires that those who believe in Him succeed and be victorious in life.

The Kingdom Jesus is delivering back to the earth would conquer the plans of the enemy of our souls. Believers have the opportunity to embrace a life that would give us more than enough.

CHAPTER 25

Enemies of Jesus

Although Jesus performed wonderful miracles and gave people hope and encouraged them, there were those who regarded Jesus as a threat and an enemy. Who could possibly not like Jesus? It was those who knew the scriptures best, the Pharisees and the Sadducees. These were men who thought they guarded the Law of Moses and it was their duty to adhere to them. Unfortunately the Law of Moses that God gave had been enhanced, embellished and even perverted over hundreds of years. Using men, the law was perverted by the enemy to benefit those who professed to be the leaders of the synagogue and give them power over people. This would cause disillusionment and confusion among the those that God loved so much.

Jesus defied the laws the men had made. These added laws made His Father's Laws and statutes' so binding that it was difficult to understand His love. Jesus' whole purpose for coming to the earth was to demonstrate God's heart and His love to His creation. With the self-imposing rules of the religious sect, it made the love of God obscure and impersonal, even cold. Jesus needed to let the rabbi's and scribes know how they looked to the Father. Often the Pharisees would stand among the crowd and listen to Jesus. Then they would ask Him a question to try to trip Him up. Jesus knew what they were up to and wasn't surprised when they pulled the ultimate trick on Him.

There was a political party called the Herodians who, on any normal day would be an enemy of the Pharisees. But because both groups wanted to see Jesus eliminated from their communities, they united for this one cause. This particular day, the Pharisees sent their students with the Herodians to Jesus to find fault in Him. The men started by saying, "Teacher, we know that You are true, and teach the way of God in truth; nor do you care about anyone, for you do not regard the person of men. Tell us, therefore, what do you think? Is it lawful to pay taxes to Caesar, or not?" They had done this before and Jesus knew it was a trick. He asked them, "Why do you test Me, you hypocrites? Show Me the tax money." So they brought Him a denarius. Jesus asked, "Whose image and inscription is this?" as He pointed to Caesar's picture on the coin. The men said, "Caesar's." Jesus said to them, "Render therefore to Caesar the things that are Caesar's, and to God the things that are God's." This left the men in awe and because Jesus was completely honest and they found nothing in which to fault Him. (Matt. 22: 16:15-22, Mark 12:13-17)

Many times we are tempted to not pay our taxes because we don't agree with the system. But Jesus' response is that we pay our taxes to the government and we pay our tithes to God. There is no other way to please God. Honor the governmental system and honor God.

These groups of the Sadducees and Pharisees kept attending Jesus' meetings asking Him hard questions expecting Jesus to stumble somewhere but He never did. Eventually they decided that since they couldn't get Jesus to step into their traps, they would go to the Roman government and tell lies about Jesus just to get Him arrested. As this plot was being developed between the Jewish leaders and the Roman government, Jesus knew His time was short.

CHAPTER 26

Jesus' View of Wealth

There were many wealthy men and women in Jesus' life. He was supported by wealthy people and didn't reject their support. He knew it was important for them to give to Him since He was representing God on this earth. One day Jesus told a story that illustrated how important it is to use your money to benefit people and the Kingdom of Heaven. There were two men in His story, one's name was Lazarus the other was called a "certain rich man." The rich man had everything in life he needed, was dressed in fine clothes and ate wonderful rich foods. Lazarus was a beggar who sat at the rich man's gate, just looking for crumbs from the man's table. The rich man never helped the beggar who was also obviously sick.

In this story, both men died. They ended up in the place of the dead. The rich man was in a place that was hot, there was no water or food, and the torment never ended. He looked across a great gulf and saw the beggar, Lazarus that had lain at his gate, sitting in the arms of Abraham where he was enjoying a very comfortable existence.

The rich man cried out to Father Abraham "Have mercy on me and send Lazarus that he may dip the tip of his finger in water and cool my tongue; for I am tormented in this flame." But Abraham said, "Son, remember that in your lifetime you received your good things, and likewise Lazarus evil things; but now he is comforted and you are tormented. See this great gulf between us? No one can pass over this from one side to the other. Lazarus cannot get to you and you cannot come here."

The rich man then appealed to Abraham to send Lazarus back to his five living brothers to tell them of the awful place he would spend eternity because of his stinginess and lack of care for those less fortunate than he. Abraham said, "They have Moses and the prophets; let your brothers hear them." To that the rich man replied, "No, Father Abraham; but if one goes to them from the dead, they will repent." Abraham finally said to him, "If they do not hear Moses and the prophets, neither will they be persuaded through one rising from the dead." (Luke 16:19-31)

Jesus finished his story. The reason He told this was to emphasize the importance of looking at other's needs. Wealth does not automatically condemn one to hell, nor does poverty in this life guarantee eternal joy. If the rich man had compassion on Lazarus and helped him with medical needs or food, perhaps he would have spent eternity in Abraham's bosom and Heaven. Instead, he chose to overlook the needs of Lazarus.

Jesus was aware that the works of man doesn't automatically reward a person with an eternity in heaven. However if one has a relationship with God through Jesus Christ, there is a heart change that will be reflected in an attitude toward material possessions and wanting to help others. When we live to please God, we will then be happy to help those whom we can help with the possessions God has given us.

CHAPTER 27

Jesus and the Death of Lazarus

Jesus' days on the earth were coming to a close. He continued to give the gospel to the people, but He was spending more time with His closest group, the disciples. They were the ones that would continue to spread the Good News when His work was finished on the earth. Even though the disciples knew that Jesus was the Messiah, the Son of the Living God, they didn't completely understand all that Jesus taught them. Jesus knew that they would have to experience many things before they realized that the words He had spoken described what would happen.

As Jesus and the disciples were in one of those meetings in the countryside, word came to Jesus that His dearest friend, Lazarus, was very sick. His sisters Mary and Martha wanted Him to come because they knew that He could heal him. When Jesus heard the report, He said, "This sickness is not unto death, but for the glory of God, that the Son of God may be glorified through it." With that, Jesus continued to teach the disciples two more days. Finally He said, "Let us go to Judea again."

The persecution from the religious sect was getting stronger toward Jesus and their hate was influencing more and more people. The crowd tried to stone Jesus the last time He was in the area and the disciples were fearful to go back. Jesus shared another spiritual truth about fear. He said, "Are there not twelve hours in the day? If anyone walks in the day, he does not stumble because he sees the light of this world. But if one walks in the night, he stumbles, because the light is not in him." (John 11:9,10) He was referring to Himself as the day and Satan as the night. When we have the life of God on the inside of us, we should have no fear of Satan and his strategies against us.

With that, Jesus said, "Our friend Lazarus only sleeps, but I go that I may wake him up." The disciples thought Jesus meant that Lazarus was taking a rest in sleep, but Jesus was referring that he had died. So Jesus had to say, "Lazarus is dead. And I am glad for your sakes that I was not there that you may believe. Nevertheless let us go to him." The disciples must have looked at each other in dismay. They found it hard to believe that Jesus was glad that His beloved Lazarus was dead. This was truly confusing, but they followed Jesus to Bethany. They knew something spectacular was going to happen, and it did!

As Jesus arrived in Bethany, He found that Lazarus had been in the tomb for four days. Because Bethany was only two miles away from Jerusalem, many of the Jews from there had joined the sisters, Mary and Martha, to comfort them. When Martha heard that Jesus was approaching, she ran to Him while Mary remained in the house. When she reached Jesus Martha said, "Lord, if You had been here, my brother would not have died. But even now, I know that whatever You ask of God, God will give You." Her faith was so expectant that she knew that Jesus could raise Lazarus from the dead.

They continued walking to the house as Jesus said, "Your brother will rise again." Martha, knowing what she had been taught in the synagogue about the future of the resurrection of the dead in the last day said, "I know that he will rise again in the resurrection at the last day." Jesus turned to her, looking into her eyes and said, "I am the Resurrection and the Life. He who believes in Me, though he may die, he shall live. And whoever lives and believes in Me shall never die. Do you believe this?" Martha answered and said, "Yes, Lord, I believe that You are the Christ, the Son of God, who is to come into the world."

It seemed Jesus spoke in riddles, "Though he may die, he shall live?" "Whoever lives and believes in me shall never die?" It may have been very confusing, but Jesus saw beyond the natural and saw the spiritual. He was saying we may die in our physical bodies, but we can live forever with the Father in Heaven if we believe in what Jesus said and demonstrated.

As if in total communion with each other, Martha left Jesus and His group and secretly called Mary saying, "The Teacher has come and is calling for you." This was coded because of the Jews that were conspiring against Jesus that surrounded them. As soon as Mary heard this, she quickly left the house to go out to meet Jesus. When she found Him, she fell down at His feet saying, "Lord, if You had been here, my brother would not have died."

Although Jesus was all God, He was also all man. When He saw His precious Mary weeping, then more of her friends came weeping, He groaned in the spirit. As the tears welled in His eyes, He asked,

"Where have you laid him?" And He wept. They said, to Him, "Come and see."

As they walked to the tomb, the group spoke quietly among themselves. They were asking, "Couldn't this Man, who opened the eyes of the blind, also have kept this man from dying?" As Jesus came to the tomb, He became filled with an anger that came from His spirit. Here was a man, too young to die, that was again a victim of Satan's devices! One more time, Satan stole life from a young man and peace from his sisters. Satan killed a life and at the same time stole dreams. The righteous anger that filled Jesus came out and it sounded like a groan as He commanded, "Take away the stone."

Martha came to His side and said, "Lord, by this time there is a stench. He's been in that tomb four days!" Jesus said to her, "Did I not say to you that if you would believe you would see the glory of God?" Strong men took away the stone from the place where the dead man was lying. At that moment, Jesus lifted up His eyes and said, "Father, I thank You that You have heard Me. And I know that You always hear Me, but because of the people who are standing by I said this, that they may believe that You sent Me." He then cried out in a commanding voice, "Lazarus, come forth!"

Within a few minutes, from within the dark, dank tomb came a figure that was bound hand and foot with grave clothes, along with his face that was wrapped with a cloth. Jesus said to them, "Loose him and let him go." It was then that the disciples understood what Jesus had intended. Two men quickly ran up to Lazarus and unwrapped the grave clothes exposing a very alive Lazarus. Great rejoicing erupted and all glory was given to God. As a result, many of the Jews who had come to mourn with the sisters and had seen the things Jesus did, believed in Him. (John 11)

Lazarus was loosed not only from the clothes that bound him, but from the devil's plan to kill him. Jesus knew that the devil would not stop at Lazarus, for He had gone too far in exposing the evil and strategies he had toward mankind. Jesus had just demonstrated how to break the bondage of Satan. His commanding authority broke that which Satan had used to enslave mankind; sickness, brokenness, hopelessness and even death were conquered that day. Now Satan was committed to destroy Jesus and to stop His movement of empowering people which in turn would diminish his plans to destroy and kill all of mankind. There were others in the crowd that saw Lazarus come out of the tomb and they went away to the Pharisees and told them the things Jesus did.

CHAPTER 28

Satan's Plot to Remove Jesus

The chief priests and the Pharisees started meeting and planning how to stop Jesus. The "Lazarus Incident" had them shaken. Many Jews left Bethany believing Jesus was the Messiah. The priests were afraid everyone would believe in Jesus and turn from their Jewish traditions, losing their power and authority over the people. They also felt if Jesus gained more followers, the Romans would come and take away both Jerusalem and eventually the nation of Israel. So they began plotting how to eliminate Jesus. They reasoned it would be best for one man to die instead of the whole nation. This is the way Satan works. He deceives people into believing a lie.

Satan uses people. He will not reveal his own person, but empowers men through mental images and thoughts what he wants to accomplish. Jesus was not the only one that was a thorn in the side, but also anyone who becomes a follower, disciple, believer in Jesus as the Son of God. Jesus was a huge threat to Satan's dominion on the earth. Satan felt if he removed Jesus he would eliminate the threat. Little did he know he was playing right into the hand of the "divine plan." Satan cannot read minds, he is not omniscient (all knowing) as God is. He reads facial expressions, listens to our speech, watches our attitudes and of course uses our history against us.

Jesus knew his time was growing short, He started being bolder in his actions and when He taught his followers, he was more deliberate in preparing them for his future on the earth and giving them direction for their future as well.

CHAPTER 29

Darkness Closes In

Jesus knew this time was coming, a time when the religious spirit would raise its ugly head and help the Sadducees and Pharisees succeed in a plan to kill Him. The spiritual atmosphere was getting darker and darker. Even though people surrounded Him with love and adoration, those on the fringes of the crowd were plotting to kill Him. Jesus knew He must work more closely with those who had been devoted to Him for three years to prepare them for what was ahead.

Although the twelve men walked with Jesus from village to village, slept with Him under the trees, watched as He performed amazing signs and miracles, there was still a lot of teaching that needed to take place. Jesus sensed the spiritual atmosphere of evil closing in and knew He had a short time. His disciples needed more of His personal time so when He was no longer with them, they could continue His work.

One of His disciples was Judas Iscariot. He joined the troupe of disciples following Jesus because He saw that Jesus could be One that would confront the oppressive Roman government. Judas felt that Jesus could possibly start a revolution because He kept talking about a kingdom. As the years passed by, Judas began to realize that Jesus was a man of peace and love. Jesus explained that the Kingdom He was setting up was not on this earth, but in Heaven.

Judas was disappointed and deeply agitated by this because he wanted to fix the government on the earth here and now! But he realized that Jesus wasn't the one to do it. Judas kept thinking how disappointed he was in Jesus and became obsessed with those thoughts. Because he was so angry with Jesus, Satan started whispering lies into his mind. With these thoughts, Judas felt he had to force Jesus into action. In a moment when he felt overwhelmed with the need to do something, he went to the chief priests and said, "What are you willing to give me if I deliver Jesus to you?" As the priests looked at each other realizing their good fortune, they agreed to give him thirty pieces of silver when he turned over Jesus. From that time, Judas sought an opportunity to betray Him.

CHAPTER 30

The Triumphal Entry

Knowing that He had a very short time left to minister to His disciples, Jesus wanted to meet with them privately for special instructions. He asked two of His disciples to run a special errand. As they were approaching Jerusalem, He told them "Go into the village opposite you; and as soon as you have entered it you will find a colt tied, one on which no one has ever sat. Loose it and bring it to me. If anyone says to you, 'Why are you doing this?' say, 'The Lord has need of it' and immediately he will send it here." It happened exactly as He said, and they brought the colt to Jesus and threw their clothes on the animal and Jesus sat on it.

The people in the villages on the way to Jerusalem heard the Master was coming down their road. They knew of all the marvelous works He had

The Triumphal Entry

performed. Many of those who had been healed laid their clothes on the road in front of the donkey. Women who heard the One who had healed their loved ones was coming by started cutting branches from trees to lie at the feet of their Messiah. Children started waving palm fronds shouting "Hosanna! Blessed is He who comes in the name of the Lord! Blessed is the kingdom of our father David that comes in the name of the Lord! Hosanna in the highest!" (Mark 11:1-10)

> **Hosanna**
> *Save Now!*
> *Came to be a customary shout of praise like "Hallelujah"*

Jesus knew that what He was doing was the fulfillment of the prophecy of Zechariah which said, *"Rejoice greatly, O daughter of Zion! Shout, O daughter of Jerusalem! Behold your King is coming to you; He is just and having salvation, lowly and riding on a donkey, a colt, the foal of a donkey."* (Zechariah 9:9)

Judas, was appalled at the lowly way Jesus was presenting Himself. Although he knew Jesus wasn't going to meet his expectations in the way He would conquer the Romans, he still was embarrassed at how Jesus was presenting Himself.

"How can anyone be a conqueror riding on a donkey", Judas thought! "Kings should ride a stallion and prance in the glory of knowing He would be the victor over the Romans!" His thoughts continued, "Jesus looks ridiculous. He will be the laughing stock of all the city of Jerusalem." More of these thoughts flooded the mind of Judas which made him angrier and angrier. But in the week ahead, Jesus would accomplish all that He had come to earth to do. He would deliver the Kingdom of God to the earth through one act of sacrifice.

CHAPTER 31

More to Teach

Just as parents who are about to leave their children for a trip or an employer who is about to leave the business to his employees for a time, the most important last minute instructions are spoken as they depart. Jesus did the same with His disciples. There were many things that He wanted to convey to them in a short time. So over the last few days of His life, He started telling them the harder, deeper things of faith and their future.

Following Jesus' triumphal entrance into Jerusalem, He started teaching His disciples how to speak in faith. The day before, He had been hungry and wanted a fig, but the tree they found was producing no figs because it was not the season. Even so, Jesus declared, "Let no one eat fruit from you ever again." The disciples heard this and

More to Teach

looked at each other confused, thinking He was just grumpy.

The next morning, they passed by the same fig tree and saw that it had dried up at the roots. Peter said, "Look Rabbi! The fig tree you cursed has withered away!" Jesus, knowing this was an object lesson He had to teach, began by saying, "Have faith in God! Listen to Me." Pointing to a nearby hill, Jesus said, "Whoever says to this mountain, 'Be removed and be cast into the sea' and really believes what he says and doesn't doubt in his heart, it will be done. When you believe that God hears you and you are speaking according to the heart of God, then I say to you, whatever things you ask when you pray, believe that you receive them and you will have them." (Mark 11:20-24)

Jesus knew that His physical presence with the disciples would be over. They would soon be on their own and had to know how to take authority in the spiritual realm to make a difference with things in the natural realm. Jesus wanted them to realize that faith and doubt are the exact opposites. If one has any doubt in their heart, they are expressing that God doesn't exist or that He is unloving and uncaring about your needs. Doubt, Jesus knew, gives rise to fear, which brings torment, not peace. Fear, Satan's number one weapon against the human mind, actually keeps men from receiving the good things God desires to send their way.

"Oh," Jesus thought, "if mankind could only know how much My Father loves them. He wants to give them good things and not bad. What parent would give a child a stone instead of bread? My Father is a wonderful parent to all who would just believe! He has so many good things stored up for them if they would just believe and have faith."

CHAPTER 32

Jesus Celebrates Passover with His Disciples

The time to celebrate the Feast of the Unleavened Bread had arrived. Jesus told them to go to a certain man and say to him, "The Teacher says, 'My time is at hand; I will keep the Passover at your house with My disciples.'" So the preparation was accomplished and when evening had come, Jesus sat down with the twelve. These were the twelve that had been with him for the last three years; walking, sleeping, eating and experiencing the miraculous hand of God wherever He went.

Usually a servant would wash the feet of the guests when they enter a home. But, since they were meeting privately, there were no servants at the moment. Jesus removed His tunic and took a towel and bowl of water. He then asked the disciples to remove their sandals so He could wash their feet.

Jesus Celebrates Passover with His Disciples

Peter spoke up and said to Him, "Lord, are You washing my feet?" Jesus answered and said, "What I am doing you do not understand now, but you will know after this night." Then Peter said, "You shall never wash my feet!" He said this because he knew Jesus was the Son of God. He felt they should be washing His feet.

Jesus answered him, "If I do not wash you, you have no part of Me." Then Peter said with humor, "OK, don't stop at my feet, wash my hands and head, too." Jesus finished washing all their feet, then when He was done He asked, "Do you know what I have done for you? You think I shouldn't lower Myself because of who I am. But I have given you an example that you should do as I have done to you. Listen to Me. Servanthood should be expressed by all, whether you have a high or low position. No one is higher than another. This is a lesson all must learn.

Just as the meal was being served, Jesus said, "Listen to Me, one of you will betray Me." Each one looked at the other with a question in their eyes. They each turned to Jesus and asked, "Lord, is it I?" Judas and Jesus had just reached for the same bowl to dip their bread when He made that statement. Everyone was so shocked they hadn't noticed and Jesus simply said, "It is the one who dipped his hand with Me in the dish who will betray Me. The Son of Man indeed goes just as it is written of Him, but woe to that man by whom the Son of Man is betrayed! It would have been good for that man if he had not been born." Even Judas played along and said, "Rabbi, is it I?" And Jesus said, "You have said it." Now after dipping the piece of bread, Satan entered him. Then Jesus said to him, "What you do, do quickly." With that, Judas left the room to go to the priests waiting to hear where they might find Jesus. (Matthew 26:17-25) (John 13:27)

The disciples didn't think it out of the ordinary that Judas would leave since he was often running errands for the Master. However, on this night, Judas was running an errand for Satan.

CHAPTER 33

A New Covenant

As the meal was being completed, Jesus said "I have really looked forward to this time with you before I submit Myself to My enemies." He then took bread and broke it saying, "Take and eat, this is My body." Then He took the cup and when He had given thanks He gave it to them, and they all drank from it. Jesus said to them, "This is my blood of the new covenant, which is shed for many for the remission of sins."

> **Remission**
> *Freedom, pardon, deliverance, forgiveness, liberty*

Although those elements weren't really Jesus' body or blood, they were to be a symbol for all to remember a new covenant that Jesus was creating to take the place of the old covenant that was established in the past. Not until Jesus completed

His assignment on earth would anyone, even the disciples, understand the New Covenant. (Matthew 26:26-28)

Jesus continued talking with His dearest friends. "Little children, I shall be with you a little while longer. You will seek Me; and as I said before, where I am going you cannot come, so now I say to you; A new commandment I give to you, that you love one another; as I have loved you, that you also love one another. By this all will know that you are My disciples, if you have love one for another." (John 13:33-35)

Jesus let His mind wander back to the day He had been asked by the scribes listening to Him teach, "Which is the first commandment of all?" Jesus, knowing that this group really wanted to know and wasn't trying to trick Him answered, "The first of all the commandments is 'Hear, O Israel, the Lord our God, the Lord is one. And you shall love the Lord your God with all your heart, with all your soul and with all your mind and with all your strength.' This is the first commandment. And the second is like it. It is this: You shall love your neighbor as yourself. There is no other commandment greater than these." (Mark 12:28-31)

"Love," Jesus thought, "is the glue that holds this world together. Satan wants hate to infiltrate the mortar of this world. If people could love each other, then there would be consistent care, thought and dedication between people of all races and creeds. Oh, that my sacrifice would be recognized as the ultimate love for all mankind." With that last thought, Jesus shook Himself back to reality.

CHAPTER 34

The Holy Spirit Revealed

With His closest disciples gathered in the Upper Room, Jesus revealed a very special part of a sad message. He had been telling those who had been with Him for years that He was going to leave them, but this time Jesus wanted to give them a message of hope. He said, "I have been sharing many things with you in the past. But the Helper, the Holy Spirit, Whom the Father will send in My name, He will teach you all things and help you remember everything I have told you. I am leaving you a special gift and that of Peace. My peace is a different kind of peace that this world doesn't hold. Don't be troubled and don't be afraid."

"You have heard me say that I am going away and then coming back to you. If you loved Me you would rejoice because I am going to the Father. I'm telling you this before it happens so that when it does, you will believe. I don't have much more time with you because the ruler of this world is coming, but he has nothing on Me. The world will know that I love the Father and as the Father gives Me a commandment, I will do it." He then called to His disciples. "Come, let us go to the Garden to pray." (John 14:27-31)

Jesus knew that Satan was about to have his way with Him. He knew that Satan felt the only way to keep his dominion on the earth was to kill Jesus. Jesus, his enemy, was influencing too many people and giving them knowledge of power and dominion over Satan and his demons. Jesus knew if those people told their friends and family about His life and the love He had for others, this would multiply and make more people aware of the power of the Kingdom of Heaven.

The message that Jesus was spreading was infiltrating the hearts and minds of Jews making many converts. These Jews realized life could be more enjoyable and prosperous through the life of Jesus Christ. Satan had to force his way into the minds of those who were already threatened by Jesus and work his deceitful plan.

Men were obeying Satan and his demons by giving in to hate and greed. That very night, Judas gave the priests the information they needed as to where to find Jesus and received the thirty pieces of silver he was promised. The priests then made arrangements with the government to arrest Jesus in the garden while others were spreading lies and rumors about Him. The plan was to incite the people against Jesus so when He was before the governor, they would rise up against Him.

Jesus, as the Son of God and the Son of Man, knew what was happening in both spiritual worlds. He knew what Judas had done and He also knew that Satan had organized a conspiracy among the Pharisees to turn Him over to the Roman government. There had been several plots to remove Jesus and even to kill Him, but those efforts were early in His ministry and could not be accomplished. Now, at this time, Jesus was ready to give Himself over to those who hated Him. It was for this time that Jesus came to the earth. This was the ultimate sacrifice Jesus would make for mankind.

He knew it would be very difficult for His humanness, but He also knew the Holy Spirit would be there to give Him the strength to face the next several hours. "The Holy Spirit," Jesus thought, "will be My strength and comfort. He will be with Me every step of the way."

CHAPTER 35

Final Instructions

As they were walking to the garden, Jesus wanted to share some very special instructions to His remaining eleven disciples. Jesus began by saying, "I want you to think of Me as the Vine and my Father as the Vinedresser. Every branch that is attached to Me that does not bear fruit, He will take away. If the branch does bear fruit, He will prune it so that it can bear more fruit. I am the Vine, you are the branches. He who abides in Me, and I in him, bears much fruit for without Me you can do nothing." If anyone does not abide in Me, he is cast out as a branch and is withered, then they will collect that branch and throw it into the fire and they are burned. If you abide in Me, and My words abide in you, you will ask what you desire, and it shall be

> **Abide**
> *Dwell, remain, set roots down as in a foundation*

done for you. My Father is glorified when you bear much fruit. (John 15:1-8)

The disciples nodded and agreed that what Jesus had just said made sense. They talked among themselves a few minutes about what fruit they would bear. Then Jesus said, "You have seen how the Father loves Me. I also have loved you, dwell in My love. If you keep My commandments, you will abide in My love, just as I have kept My Father's commandments and abide in His love. I have told you these things so that My joy will remain in you and that your joy will be full. This is My commandment: That you love one another as I have loved you. Greater love has no one than this, to lay down one's life for his friends and you are My friends. So go and do whatever I command you. (John 15:9-13)

Jesus and the disciples continued to walk and He told them many things to come. He told them that they didn't choose Him, but He chose them and appointed them to go and bear fruit and that their fruit would remain. He also told them that whatever they asked the Father in His Name He would give them. Then He told them of how the world will hate them because of who they had become. They would be witnesses to all people, telling them who Jesus was and the Holy Spirit would help them.

CHAPTER 36

The Coming of the Holy Spirit

Jesus started to get excited when He began talking about the Holy Spirit. He talked as if the Holy Spirit was His friend and companion. As the disciples approached the hill of Gethsemane where they were going to pray, Jesus started talking more of His leaving.

"I know you are growing sad because I keep talking about going away, but I have to tell you, it is to your advantage that I leave, because if I don't, the Holy Spirit, Who is your Helper, will not come. But when I leave, I will send Him to you. Just as the Father and I are One, so is the Holy Spirit and I, One. I am only one person, but the Holy Spirit can be a Helper to each one of you, all at the same time."

The Coming of the Holy Spirit

"When He, the Holy Spirit has come, He will convict the world of sin and of righteousness and of judgment. Of sin because they do not believe in Me, of righteousness because I go to My Father and you will see Me no more; and of judgment, because the ruler of this world, Satan, is judged."

> **Righteousness**
> *To be equal in character or actions; just as if you had never sinned*

"There are so many things I want to share, but I don't think you can handle them right now. But when He, the Spirit of Truth, has come, He will guide you into all truth, for He will not speak on His own authority, but whatever He hears He will speak; and He will tell you things to come. He will honor and glorify Me, for He will take of what is Mine and declare it to you. All things that the Father has are Mine. Therefore, the Holy Spirit will take what is Mine and declare it to you." (John 16:5-15)

> **Declare**
> *Report, share, tell, show*

This is why Jesus came…to make it possible for God to work through all of mankind to overrule the works of Satan. The Holy Spirit who resided in Jesus would not be with man until Jesus had returned to Heaven. Jesus was overjoyed at the thought of the precious Holy Spirit coming to live in everyone who would receive the Good News message. He was especially pleased that all the authority and power that He held as the Son of God would also be available to all believers.

The more Jesus talked about the Holy Spirit, the more excited He became. It was if He really wanted to go away and leave the disciples in the care of the Holy Spirit. One of the disciples spoke out his observation that Jesus appeared to want to leave them so the Holy Spirit could come. Jesus responded, "I am only one man and can speak to only a few of you at once. But when the Holy Spirit comes, He will be able to speak to everyone on the earth at the same time, be everywhere at the same time and give anyone who believes in Me the authority to do the mighty works I did. It is good that I leave you so One so mighty can come." "Ahh, here we are," said Jesus. They were just approaching the beautiful olive groves located in a garden where Jesus and the men liked to pray.

Before the men split up to pray in their separate areas, Jesus called them all together. "It won't be long now," Jesus said, "you won't see Me, then you will see Me because I will go to the Father." (John 16:16) Here He was again, speaking in riddles; "You won't see Me then you will see me..." The men that surrounded Him had been with Him for several years, but never heard Him talk like that before. They looked at each other questioning what He meant. "What does He mean by a little while?" they asked each other.

Knowing that they had a question about this, Jesus said, "Are you asking yourselves about what I said? Let me tell you, I know you will weep and lament, but the world will rejoice; and you will be sorrowful for a while, but then joy will come in the morning." "Look at a woman in labor, she is sorrowful and weeping, but when the baby has arrived, she is full of joy and forgets the pain and anguish in giving birth to the child."

"The same will happen to you, but remember the darkness will turn to light. In that day you will ask Me nothing. But listen, I am telling you, whatever you ask the Father in My name He will give you. Until now, you have asked nothing in My name. Ask and you will receive that your joy may be full." (John 16:16-24)

CHAPTER 37

Jesus Asks God to Deliver Him From This Hour

"Go now and pray. Peter, James and John, stay with me as I go into the alcove." The disciples saw Jesus' whole demeanor change. Where He was buoyant and excited as He talked about the Holy Spirit, He was now sorrowful and deeply distressed. He said to them, "My soul is exceedingly sorrowful, even to death. Stay here and watch with Me."

He left His dearest friends and went a little further and fell on His face in prayer "Oh My Father, if it is possible, let this cup pass from Me. However it is not My will, but Your will that must be done." After He had prayed a little more, Jesus returned to the three men He left to watch. Finding them sleeping, Jesus nudged Peter awake saying, "What? Could you not watch with Me one hour?" "Watch and pray so you don't enter into temptation. I

Jesus Asks God to Deliver Him From This Hour

know your spirit is willing, but the flesh is weak." With that He left the men to return to His place of prayer.

Again, Jesus prayed to His Father asking if there was any other way that mankind could be redeemed from their sin and separation from the God Who created them. But knowing He was the only One who could satisfy that separation, Jesus prayed for strength for the coming hours. It was while He was praying that an angel of the Lord came to be with Him. He was in such agony and prayed so hard that His sweat became like great drops of blood falling down to the ground. When He returned to the men, again they were sleeping. "Are you still sleeping?" Jesus asked. Pointing to the road that lead up to the garden He said, "Look, it is time because the Son of Man is being betrayed into the hands of sinners. Get up, see? My betrayer is here." (Matthew 26:36-46; Luke 22:39-46)

The rest of the disciples gathered around Jesus as they looked down the hill to see not only priests, but Roman soldiers with torches to light the path and swords strapped to their sides and clubs in their hands. The closer they got, the louder their voices grew. Jesus and his men then recognized among the chief priests and scribes one of their own, Judas Iscariot. When they arrived to the grove, Judas walked up to Jesus and gave Him a kiss on each cheek. This was the signal to the soldiers which of the men was to be arrested. Jesus said to him, "Judas, are you betraying the Son of Man with a kiss?"

The disciples were upset and angry when they realized Jesus was being arrested. Peter had a sword with him and to defend Jesus he drew it and sliced the ear off one of the chief priests' servant. Putting up His hand, Jesus said, "We have to allow this." Jesus knew this was the will of the Father, that it had been prophesied hundreds of years before. It was now time for it to be accomplished.

The man was screaming with pain holding his head where the ear had once been. With great compassion, Jesus picked up the ear of the servant and placed it back where it belonged, healing it as though it had never happened. Then Jesus said to the chief priests and everyone from the temple, "You come out here with clubs and swords like you are coming for a thief. Here, I was in your temple every day and you didn't try to seize me then. But now that it is dark and no one can see, you come after me." (Luke 22:47-53)

Jesus Asks God to Deliver Him From This Hour

As the soldiers tied Jesus' hands, knowing that Jesus would not struggle, the disciples fled into the dark of the night, confused and frightened. They were terrified that they could also be arrested.

CHAPTER 38

Trial and Denial

Jesus was taken from the grove to the home of the High Priest, Caiaphas. The house was full of other priests, scribes and elders, also known as the Sanhedrin council, as they waited for the prisoner. The disciples scattered not wanting to be arrested themselves, but it was Peter who followed at a distance to watch after his Master. When he came to the courtyard, a group of people were milling around who were curious about the events taking place.

Peter found himself by the fire trying to blend in, his thoughts whirling, confused and frightened at what appeared to be a trial of some kind. "What a turn of events," Peter thought, "We weren't doing anything! Why would anyone want to hurt Jesus? He simply wants to love and help everyone. What is going to happen?" As he sat in the courtyard

Trial and Denial

gazing into the embers of the fire, a young girl came up, pointed to him and declared, "You were also with this Jesus of Galilee." Those around the fire looked over to her then turned to look at him. Peter, shocked that anyone would recognize him, said the first thing that came out of his mouth, "I don't know what you are talking about."

Peter got up from the fire to get away from the searching eyes and walked to a gate. He wanted to stay near Jesus, but didn't need any attention drawn to him. "I certainly don't need to get myself arrested," he thought.

Meanwhile inside the house, with hands bound behind His back, Jesus was standing in front of all the priests, scribes and elders. It was an austere group of men, all in their formal priestly robes. They were called to this hastily formed hearing with the intent to cast guilt on this innocent man. Although the priests had tried to find some folks that could give testimony even if it was false, they couldn't find anyone whose testimonies would agree. But finally, with some searching, they found two witnesses who would exaggerate the truth, even then their testimony didn't agree. Finally with exasperation at having no witnesses to come against Jesus, the high priest named Caiaphas, stood up among all the men and asked Jesus, "Why don't you answer the charges against You?" Jesus kept silent and didn't answer anyone. Then the same priest asked Him, "Are You the Christ, the Son of the Blessed?"

Jesus finally answered saying, "I am. And you will see the Son of Man sitting at the right hand of the Power, and coming with the clouds of heaven." Then the high priest tore his clothes saying, "He has spoken blasphemy!" Then looking around the room Caiaphas asked, "What do you think?" And they all in one way or another declared "Death to Him!"

Outside, while standing at the gate, a man came by looking at Peter. The man said, "This fellow was also with Jesus of Nazareth!" Peter said in a loud voice, "I don't know the Man!" At the end of the courtyard, a rooster crowed, although not unusual, to Peter, it sounded like a piercing horn

After the court finished, guards played a game with Him blindfolding and striking Him and then asking Jesus to prophesy and tell who had hit Him. After an hour had passed, Jesus was roughly pushed and dragged out of the house, His eyes swollen and face bloody.

Peter, standing in the shadows, saw His Master and at the same time another confidently affirmed saying, "I know for certain this fellow was with Him, for his language is Galilean." Again the rooster crowed. At the same time Jesus, as He was pushed again, looked over and caught Peter's eye. It was then that Peter remembered the word Jesus spoke to Him that very evening saying, "Before the rooster crows twice, you will deny Me three times." With that, Peter fled the courtyard weeping bitterly. (Mark 14:53-72)

CHAPTER 39

Rome Tries Jesus

By this time it was morning and the plot to kill Jesus had advanced. Although Jesus knew this was going to happen, no human could comprehend the terror and pain He was experiencing. Jesus was all God, but He was also all man. His face was stretched tight with swelling from the beating He had experienced at the hands of the priests' servants and leaders. Now He was bound and being delivered to Pontius Pilate, the Governor of Judea.

The religious leaders wanted Jesus dead, but they couldn't make that happen without a real cause. So, by taking Jesus to the Roman Governor, they could bring charges that Jesus would try to cause an uprising in the nation by telling the people not to pay their taxes to Caesar, and that He was Christ, a King. Standing in front of Pilate, he asked Jesus,

Rome Tries Jesus

"Are You the King of the Jews?" Jesus answered him saying, "It is as you say. My kingdom is not of this world. If My kingdom were in this world, My servants would fight so that I should not be delivered to the Jews, but My kingdom is not from here."

Pilate then asked, "Are you a king then?" Jesus responded, "You are right that I am a King. For this cause, I was born and for this cause I have come into the world, that I should bear witness to the truth. Everyone who is of the truth hears My voice." Pilate then asked, "What is truth?" Although Jesus didn't answer, Pilate went to the priests gathered outside the chamber and said, "I find no fault in Him at all." The people waiting to hear what charges Pilate would find in Jesus were angry. They continued to accuse Jesus of many false things then someone in the crowd mentioned that Jesus had come from Galilee. When Pilate heard that, he knew that Herod was in town and that Jesus came from his jurisdiction. So, with one command, Jesus was sent to see Herod who could judge His case.

Herod had heard a lot about Jesus and had wanted to meet Him for a long time. He had even hoped to see Him perform a miracle. But when he questioned Jesus over and over, Jesus just stood there silent. The priests and scribes continued to accuse Him with great hatred. In frustration, not finding any valid charges, Herod turned Jesus over to his men of war. As with the treatment in the court with the priests, the soldiers gave Jesus another beating. They continued to treat Jesus with contempt and mocked Him by placing a beautiful robe on His shoulders. They had heard that He called Himself a king, so they wanted to make sure He had the robe of a king. Then they sent Him back to Pilate. (Luke 23:6-12 paraphrased)

CHAPTER 40

Pilate Sentences Jesus

Once again, Jesus was standing before Pilate, only this time they were both standing on a dais overlooking a swelling crowd. Word was out that Jesus, the Christ, the Messiah, was being tried as a criminal. Pilate, speaking to the High Priest and his whole council said, "After examining this man in your presence, I have found no fault in this man concerning those things you have accused Him of. I sent Him to Herod and he also found no fault in Him. He is back here and certainly does not deserve death. I will then chastise Him and then release Him." Pilot paused, and then continued "I have decided to honor your custom during Passover and release someone to you. Do you want me to release to you the King of the Jews?"

The priest and scribes were located throughout the crowd anticipating this move by Pilate. When

Pilate Sentences Jesus

Pilate asked if he could release Jesus, the scribes started shouting, "No give us Barabbas!" Barabbas was a thief and murderer and was conspiring to overthrow the government. Following the initial shouts of the scribes, the people began chanting, "Barabbas, release Barabbas!" Pilate shouted over the crowd and asked, "What do you want me to do with this man?" Again, they shouted, "Crucify Him, Crucify Him!" The crowd got louder and louder shouting, "Crucify Him!" Shocked, Pilate cried out, "Why, what has He done?" But they cried out all the more shouting, "Let Him be crucified."

Among the crowd were the followers of Jesus who had heard about the terrible turn of events. They were crying and shouting to those next to them, "No, no, let Jesus go!" But the crowd grew even louder. Standing on the edge of the crowd was Judas, the betrayer. He was appalled at what was happening to Jesus. He thought they would just chastise Him and let Him go. He didn't think it would get to this! With great remorse, Judas silently slipped away from the crowd and went to hang himself.

Pilate, seeing that he couldn't change their minds and couldn't risk a riot breaking out, took water and washed his hands before the crowd saying, "I am innocent of the blood of this person who has committed no crime. And the people answered and said, "His blood be on us and on our children." Pilate then released Barabbas and ordered Jesus to be beaten then crucified. (Luke 23:13-25 paraphrased)

The Roman soldiers took Jesus into the grounds of the barracks and gathered the whole garrison around Him. Jesus was stripped and a scarlet robe was draped over His shoulders. One of the men twisted a crown of thorns and beat it on His head and placed a reed in His right hand. Then in unison, they bowed their knees before Him and mockingly worshipped Him saying, "Hail, King of the Jews!" They then spat on Him, ripped off the robe, tied Him to a post and flogged Him with thirty-nine strikes. (Matthew 27:27-31; Mark 15:16-20)

The man whose job it was to flog a prisoner was an expert at his work. He knew exactly where to place the lashes to do the most damage. His whip was designed to tear the skin off a man's back. The ends of the leather held pieces of glass and metal, so with each strike of the whip on Jesus' legs, back and arms the wounds got deeper and deeper. His face was swollen and bloodied from the beating He had already had. Minute by minute Jesus was getting weaker and weaker. Blood was flowing

Pilate Sentences Jesus

from His wounds until the sand beneath His feet was red.

When the flogging was done, the soldiers grabbed Jesus and untied Him from the post. So weak, the men had to hold Jesus up until He could stand on His own. Most men would have died under such treatment, but Jesus had a job to do. He couldn't give in to death yet! His Father had given Him a commandment and with God's help, Jesus would complete the task.

CHAPTER 41

The Cross

Crucifixion was a relatively new form of punishment. Only Rome used nailing human beings to a cross until they died. It was meant to torture the condemned man, making it the worst way to die. The cross on which Jesus would hang was a pole designed to be tall enough that His feet could not touch the ground and had a cross piece in which to lay out the arms. The cross itself weighed more than a man and the trip to the crucifixion site was up hill.

Jesus tried to carry the cross along the rough streets, but crumbled to the ground every few meters. As Jesus stumbled through the town, people began following and women mourned and lamented Him. Because of the loss of blood, Jesus grew weaker with every step. As the crowd grew one of the soldiers grabbed a man from Cyrene

The Cross

named Simon to carry the cross for Jesus. The hill on which the crucifixions were held was called Golgotha, meaning 'Place of the Skull.' (Luke 23:26,27; Mark 15:21; Matthew 27:32)

On that day, there were two other men condemned to die by crucifixion. Each man was placed on either side of Jesus. The soldiers were quick with their work. They tore off Jesus' clothes and laid Him on the cross that was lying on the ground. Spikes were used to nail each hand stretched out to either side of His body and His feet were laid on top of each other and nailed to the cross. To stand the cross, there was a hole in the ground deep enough to keep it from tipping forward. Finished, the soldiers lifted the cross upright and tipped it into the hole. It fell hard, jarring the nearly unconscious Jesus to respond with a scream of pain. The two men on either side were treated the same way.

The crowd had followed Jesus up the hill which included Jesus' followers. Among them was His mother, Mary. Other women that had tended to Jesus were also there with emotions ranging from anger to horror to hopelessness. "How could this happen? Why didn't someone stop this?" they asked one another. Weeping silently a short distance away was Mary who had borne this man, knowing He was the promised Messiah of the people of Abraham, Isaac and Jacob. She knew His mission was one of sacrifice, but she never imagined it would end in this horrific way. As she looked up to her Son and saw His battered body, she cried out to God to stop this insanity.

It was then that Jesus looked down on the crowd and said, "Father, forgive them for they don't know what they are doing." (Luke 23:34) It took all of Jesus' strength to get those words out, but within Him, He knew it was necessary to forgive those who had schemed and plotted against Him. The Roman soldiers had picked up on the dark, vile atmosphere that Satan and his minions had created in the courtyard of the governor. Some were taunting and cursing Jesus, but there were a few that couldn't figure out why this man was being crucified. But, they reasoned, they were under orders.

The people around Jesus were ignorant of this deception and wickedness that pervaded the earth. They were looking on with conflicting thoughts. Even the rulers of the synagogue sneered saying, "He saved others; let Him save Himself if He is the Christ, the chosen of God." (Luke 23:35) Although He had the authority to stop these events, Jesus knew He had to stay on the cross. It was Satan who was behind this plot to kill Him not the religious community. Hanging on the cross, Jesus knew without this ultimate sacrifice mankind would remain in this corrupt, evil state and be doomed forever. Right now, they were without a relationship with their Creator. In a few more days, all men and women would have the opportunity to receive that relationship.

Invisible to the people on the hill, Satan was beside himself with glee. Watching the whole spectacle he said to the demons next to him, "We have caught ourselves the Son of God. He's pinned to that pole like a stuck pig! HaHaHa!" All the demons around him laughed thinking they finally got their nemesis, their arch enemy. "Yeah, go ahead and die, JESUS, you're not going anywhere. You'll just rot in the tomb like everyone else!" they snarled.

The soldiers that nailed Him to the cross had to stay on the site until the prisoners died, so they decided to make a sport of Jesus' tunic, casting lots to see which man would carry home the prize. Little did they know they were fulfilling a prophecy that said, *"They divided My garments among them and for My clothing they cast lots." (Psalm 22:18)* The soldiers had also put a sign over Jesus' head with the accusation written against

Him: THIS IS JESUS THE KING OF THE JEWS. (Matthew 27:35-37)

As time went by, one of the two thieves started taunting Jesus saying, "You, who destroy the temple and build it in three days, save Yourself. If You are the Son of God, come down from the cross." Jesus just looked at him and tried to push up on his feet so He could get a breath. With little strength and great pain, all the weight on His feet made it hard to push up to catch a breath. His breathing was laborious as His lungs were filling up with fluid because His heart could not pump the blood normally. Jesus was dying.

When the other thief heard what the other criminal said to Jesus, he said, "Don't you even fear God since you are in the same circumstance? We deserve what we are getting, but this Man has done nothing wrong." Then he said to Jesus, "Lord, remember me when You come into Your Kingdom." Jesus turned to him and said, "Assuredly, I say to you, today you will be with Me in Paradise." (Luke 23:39-43)

CHAPTER 42

The Death of Jesus

Jesus knew He was dying and started looking at the crowd. There, He saw His mother with His beloved disciple, John. With a voice barely a whisper, He said to His mother, "Woman, behold your son!" Then He said to John, "Behold your mother!" (John 19:25-27) Jesus wanted to make sure that His mother was taken care of so He put her in the care of John. From that day forward, John made sure Mary had all she needed and she lived in the comfort of his home.

After making sure His mother would be cared for, Jesus knew all He was to do had been accomplished. His assignment was finished. The people had heard of the Kingdom of God. They had seen the love of God as He walked from village to village healing, teaching and caring about everyone that He saw. Now, unknown to all those people below Him on the hill, He was doing much more. He was also taking on all the sin of mankind and all their sickness. His final task was to absorb the anguish and torment of all the sin of mankind; Pride, Envy, Hate, Fear, Covetousness, Murder, Sexual Perversion, and much more. Jesus took on Himself the sinful nature of mankind to bridge the gulf between them and their Creator.

Whatever sickness people had in their bodies He now bore. The thirty-nine stripes Jesus received at the whipping post that tore His body apart, was prophetic. There are thirty-nine basic diseases in the world today and Jesus took those diseases upon Himself so mankind would no longer have to bear them. The crown that was beat upon His head, also showed that He had taken on all our mental torment that the devil and his demons would bring against man's mind. Now, those who accepted Him and the Kingdom of God would have the authority to cast down the thoughts and imaginations Satan would send.

As Jesus hung there on the cross, His body and mind writhed with pain and agony, not only because of His wounds, but because of all our sins and sicknesses and torment. Finally, Jesus cried out in a loud voice, "My God, My God, why have You left Me?" (Matthew 27:45, 46) Jesus was in a panic because He felt no comfort from God. God had to turn His face from Jesus, remove Himself from this moment because He could not look at sin and Jesus had become Sin. Our sin. Without God, Jesus was dark and hopeless.

After knowing that all things were now accomplished, that the Scripture might be fulfilled, Jesus muttered, "I thirst." A vessel full of sour wine was sitting there and the soldiers filled a sponge with the wind, put it on hyssop and put it to His mouth. He drew a mouthful from the sponge, and then spit it out. (John 19:28,29)

When Jesus cried out in His darkest moment, people thought He was calling to Elijah. They thought maybe Elijah would rescue Him. They were waiting for something to happen, and it did. With all the strength He could muster, Jesus said with a determined voice, "It - Is - Finished" Seconds later with His last breath, He said in a loud voice, "Father, into Your hands I commit My spirit." (John 19:30; Luke 24:46)

Even though it was still day, the sky became very dark; as dark as night. The earth trembled and the mountain rock split open. Tombs opened and the bodies of many godly men and women who had died were raised from the dead. At the same time,

The Death of Jesus

in the temple in town, the great veil in the hall that closed off the holy of holies from the inner room was torn in two from the top to bottom.

In the spirit realm, a great victory had been accomplished. The veil was sixty feet tall and four inches thick. No human hand could possibly tear the curtain that thick sixty feet from the floor. It was God who rent the veil in two to demonstrate that mankind now had direct access to Him. No longer did anyone who wanted to commune with God have to go through a priest. Now man could have a direct relationship with the Creator God, the God of the universe because His Son, Jesus had been obedient and sacrificed himself for the sake of man.

The centurion at the foot of the cross looked up and said, "Truly this was the Son of God!" (Matthew 27:51-54) The crowds were shaking and greatly afraid. "Could this really be the Son of God?" they asked each other. The women from Galilee who had tended to Jesus during the three years He ministered in the villages were there watching the whole thing. A huddle of women surrounded Mary, the mother of Jesus as the crowd thinned out. As the body was gently lowered from the cross, Mary tenderly took Jesus into her lap and held Him as a little baby. Looking into His face, she remembered her little boy skipping and playing with the other children. She recalled how He seemed to love everyone and wanted to help them with their problems.

Mary's thoughts took her back to when Joseph, her husband had died. Jesus seemed to be beyond grief. He wanted to do so much more to change the circumstances, but didn't seem to know how. Mary continued thinking, "Little did He know the lives He was going to touch by healing their minds, emotions and bodies and even raising the dead back to life." The lifeless man she held in her arms was born under special circumstances, lived a life of pure love and gave to anyone who had a need. Looking into the face of death, it all seemed to be for nothing.

Now a good and just man named Joseph from Arimathea was also a part of the Sanhedrin council. He was also waiting for the Kingdom of God and believed that Jesus was the Messiah. He did not agree with the other priests of the Sanhedrin and approached Pilate for permission to bury Jesus in his tomb located nearby. Since this was the night before the Sabbath, they had to make a hasty burial.

As night was approaching, the weeping Mary let the others take Jesus and put His body on a litter to

The Death of Jesus

carry Him to the tomb. The women who had been with Jesus from Galilee followed Joseph and the body of Jesus. They saw the place where Jesus was to be buried and left to get the spices and fragrant oils to prepare Jesus' body for burial. This was to be temporary because there was not time to do it properly before the Sabbath. When the women returned, they took strips of linen and bound Jesus' body with one hundred pounds of spices as was the custom of the Jews. Weeping all the while, they honored Jesus and finished quickly and efficiently. (Luke 23:50-56; Matthew 27:57-59; Mark 15:42-47; John 19:38-42)

The next day, which followed the Day of Preparation, the chief priests and Pharisees gathered together with Pilate saying, "Sir, we remember, while He was still alive, how that deceiver (Jesus) said, 'After three days I will rise.' Therefore, command that the tomb be made secure until the third day, lest His disciples come by night and steal Him away, and say to the people, 'He has risen from the dead.' So the last deception will be worse than the first."

Pilate said to them, "You have a guard; go your way, make it as secure as you know how." So they went and made the tomb secure, sealing the stone and setting the guard. (Matthew 27:62-66)

CHAPTER 43

The Keys Regained

Jesus had died on the cross and His body was dead. The soldiers had even made sure He was dead by thrusting a sword into His side. Because it was the Preparation Day, bodies crucified, were not to remain on the cross on the Sabbath. The Jews asked Pilate that their legs might be broken and that they might be taken away. The soldiers came and broke the legs of the two thieves on either side of Jesus, but when they came to Jesus and saw that He was already dead, they did not break His legs. But one of the soldiers pierced His side with a spear, and immediately blood and water came out. (John 19:31-34 paraphrased) For these things were done that the Scripture should be fulfilled, *"Not one of His bones shall be broken."* And again another Scripture says, *"They shall look on Him whom they pierced."* (John 19:36,37)

The Keys Regained

Sealed in a cave with soldiers on watch for anything that might be amiss, Jesus' spirit was not dead. He was very much alive. As the Son of God, Jesus had been empowered to defeat death. He had been a human man, but Jesus was also God, wrapped in flesh. He was all God. Now Jesus was going to do what man could not. He was going to visit the place where Satan dwelled, Hades or better known as, Hell. Jesus was going to take back the keys of dominion that had been lost in the Garden of Eden and return them to the rightful heirs, mankind.

In hell, Satan and his angels were celebrating. They saw Jesus die on that old cross. They knew He was gone and out of their lives. Satan believed he would have free reign on the earth forever and make life even more miserable for man. "We got Him good!" shouted one slimy demon. "Yeah, I helped the man with the whip strike Him harder than usual," said another. "I was there when they drove the spikes into His hands and feet," drooled another wicked demon. "Yes, yes, yes," said Satan, but our work is just beginning!" We must put together a strategy to make the government even crueler and people more evil!" said the scheming devil. "But first, let us party! We have much to celebrate tonight. Tomorrow we will begin!"

At that moment, a bright light began to glow that made all the creatures of hell cower. They pulled their skinny arms over their eyes to shield them from an ever growing light. "What the..." began Satan, but He stopped when He saw it was the Christ, Jesus. "Satan," Jesus roared, "you thought you won, but now you will see who has Power!" "Jesus....I thought you were....," Satan sniveled" "Dead?" asked Jesus. "Oh, how you underestimate the Power of the Cross, Satan." All the demons in the chamber started gathering in a circle around the two enemies. Jesus and Satan began matching wits with each other.

"What have you to do with us?" huffed Satan. Jesus' eyes narrowed as He circled Satan and began His case. "Ever since you deceived Adam and Eve in the Garden, you have had the dominion of earth. Mankind has suffered under your rule. My Father couldn't even look on them because of the sin they bore."

"Yeeesss," smirked Satan, and his demons clapped gleefully. Jesus held up His hands to silence them and continued, "My Father has also suffered because He has been separated from His creation. Father created laws that required a blood sacrifice through animal sacrifice to redeem men from their sins, but it was only a temporary measure. They needed to be redeemed back to Him. Man couldn't do it because there was no human who was pure and holy, but I could." Jesus paused while He let His last words sink in.

> **Redeem**
> To release, preserve, rescue

Jesus, continued saying, "You are finished, Satan! I took on all the sins of all mankind, past, present and future. Father has made sure that I was the ultimate and final sacrifice. Without the shedding of innocent blood, there could be no remission of sin, but I have bought back the lives of mankind with My blood. (Hebrews 9:22) Now anyone who will believe that I came to earth through a virgin, lived a sinless life and then died on the cross..."

Satan jumped in to stop Jesus, "That's just it! You died, ha ha ha. You died!" With that all the demons cheered and made heartfelt acclamations to their leader, Satan.

"I'm not done yet," said a determined Jesus. "But you are! I have come to take back the Keys of the Kingdom! You have lost your dominion over the earth! No longer can you keep mankind enslaved!" Jesus declared. "What I have done is all that is needed to secure their freedom from your vile tyranny. I have come for those keys," Jesus said pointing to the jeweled box that held the symbol of power and authority. "I have given My life but I am not done. I have work yet to do, but you don't need to know." With that, Jesus took those coveted keys from the special place they were stored.

Just as Satan lunged for Jesus, a light that was so bright and powerful left all the demons and Satan writhing on the floor. Jesus, with the Keys of the Kingdom now in His possession, finally laughed and called to His angels to leave that vile place. Immediately, the place called hell was left in complete and total darkness, never to see light again.

As Jesus passed the place called "Abraham's Bosom," He paused to spend time there telling those who had already passed from life into death about the plan of Salvation. Those who had loved and served God since Adam and Eve, from the small to the great, had an opportunity to accept what Jesus had to tell them. Jesus then took them from that holding place and into Paradise to await the future that had been planned for mankind.

CHAPTER 44

Jesus Lives

The first day after the crucifixion, the disciples that had scattered on the night Jesus was arrested, gradually found each other. For two days, they gathered together in the upper room, in the place they had met for their last supper. Some were afraid the soldiers would come to arrest them. Others were very concerned about their future. None of them had anticipated what had transpired on Golgotha. They were confused, angry and frightened all at once. They huddled together in that private room wondering what to do with their lives. They had given so much of themselves, their time, sacrificed family and vocations to be with their Master. Now, He is gone…dead.

With the Sabbath over Mary of Magdala and another Mary were asleep in a small outcropping of rock across from the tomb where Jesus had been sealed. In the area immediately outside the tomb was a small contingent of temple soldiers who watched for anyone who might want to take the body. The priests placed them there for fear someone would steal His body for the purpose of saying He had falsely risen from the dead. A small fire kept the men warm in the dawn chill. They had been there several days and were looking forward to leaving this place of the dead to get back to the barracks for a decent sleep.

Suddenly, the ground began to quiver then shake and roll. "It's an earthquake!" shouted one of the soldiers, as they tried to remain on their feet. A brilliant light became visible to everyone around and a figure emerged, first in silhouette then in full sight. It was an angel of the Lord who had descended from Heaven and came to roll back the boulder that sealed the tomb. When he had done this, he sat on top of the huge rock.

His appearance was bright as lightening with clothing as white as snow. The soldiers were so frightened when the angel appeared, at first they were agitated, and then they could only shake in fear and eventually fell as dead men. The two women, although frightened at this amazing sight, crept toward the angel. Then they slowly bowed in the presence of this angelic being. He said to the women, "Do not be afraid, I know you are looking for Jesus who was crucified. He is not here; He has risen, just as He said He would do. Come; see the place where He lay. Then, go quickly and tell His disciples that He has risen from the dead. Tell them that Jesus has gone ahead of them to Galilee, and that they are to go there also to see Him. Behold, I have given you my message." (Matthew 28:1-7 paraphrased)

With many emotions racing through them and trembling from what they just experienced, the women ran to tell the disciples. When Mary of Magdala got to the room where the disciples were sleeping, she went to Simon Peter and John and whispered excitedly, "They have taken away the Lord out of the tomb, and we do not know where they have laid Him!" (John 20:1-2) It was difficult for Mary to share what the angel had said, for Mary was very much a human and hadn't ever experienced the appearance of an angel. She just knew that when she looked into the tomb Jesus was gone!

The disciple's response was unbelief. Where could Jesus be? Did He really rise from the dead! They thought the women were delusional and making up this story or even mad with grief. Reason told them the boulder that covered the opening was impossible to move. But it was Peter and John who got up and ran to the tomb to see for themselves. When they arrived, they too saw the stone was pushed to the side and the tomb empty.

As they peered into the tomb, they saw the linen cloths lying on the stone slab, but no body. They also saw the napkin that had wrapped His head lying, neatly folded where His head had lain. In those days, it was a social etiquette that when leaving the table while eating, to signal the servants that if you were not done and were coming back, you left a folded napkin. Peter saw the napkin recognizing the subtle sign Jesus left indicating He was coming back. Now joy filled him as he walked back to the upper room. Wonder and awe surrounded him as he thought about all that had happened. (John 20:7)

Mary Magdalene ran back to the tomb with Peter and John, but after they saw that the tomb was empty and left, Mary remained standing outside the tomb sobbing. Then, she stooped down to again to look inside the tomb and was surprised to see two angels in white sitting where the body of Jesus had laid, one at the head and one at the feet.

They said to her, "Woman, why are you crying?" Mary replied, "Because they have taken away my

Lord, and I do not know where they have laid Him." She then stood up and turned away from the tomb and saw a man standing there. Mary didn't recognize the man thinking He was the gardener, but it was actually the Messiah. Again, Jesus asked, "Woman, why are you crying? For whom are you looking?" Because she thought He was a servant, she replied, "Sir, if you carried Him away from here, tell me where you have put Him and I will take Him away."

Jesus spoke again simply saying, "Mary!" She then saw Him clearly and cried out, "Rabboni!" which means Master, or Teacher. She wanted to hug and hold Him, but He couldn't let her at that time because He wasn't finished doing things in the spirit realm yet. He said, "Do not hold Me, for I haven't ascended to the Father. But go to My brothers and tell them, I am ascending to My Father and your Father, and to My God and your God." This time, Mary took the news that she had seen the Lord to the disciples with confidence and told them everything that He had told her. (John 20:11-18)

CHAPTER 45

Jesus Appears In Person

The disciples were gathered on the same evening the stone was discovered to have been rolled away to reveal the empty tomb, only this time there was a great buzz in the room. Everyone was sharing and discussing the recent developments. Some believed the reports, others were doubtful. They were still afraid the Jewish leaders were looking for them, but somehow attitudes had changed. There was more to discuss than the finality of the death of Jesus. If He was not in the tomb, where was He? Did Mary really see and hear these things she says? What does this all mean? As they discussed and reminisced, Jesus came and stood among them and said, "Peace to you!"

There was sudden silence in the room, startled and terrified, for they thought they saw a ghost. Jesus spoke again and said, "Why are you disturbed and troubled and why do you doubt and have questions in your heart?" Jesus looked around the room at the men who had walked, talked, served and lived with Him for three years. He said, "See My hands and My feet, that it is Me! Feel free to handle Me and see, for a spirit does not have flesh and bones as you see that I have." When He said this, He pulled back the robe from His feet to reveal the holes the spikes left. He held up His hands and wrist to show the wounds left when the Roman soldiers drove those large nails to hold Him to the cross.

When they still hesitated, to lighten up the atmosphere and continue to press them to realize that it was He, Jesus asked, "Have you got anything to eat around here?" They gave Him a piece of broiled fish and He ate it in front of them. Then Jesus said, "This is what I told you would happen while I was still with you: everything that is written concerning Me in the Law of Moses and the Prophets and the Psalms must be fulfilled." (Luke 24:36-46)

Suddenly, they understood. It was like the light bulb switched on. They remembered the scriptures they learned as youths, they remembered what Jesus had taught them throughout the three years, and they remembered what Jesus said after they experienced the last supper before He was betrayed. It all flooded back to their remembrance and Jesus said to them, "Thus it is written that the Christ should suffer and on the third day rise from among the dead. (Hosea 6:2)

When the disciples "saw" the Lord, they were filled with such delight they stood up and started hugging each other. They were thrilled, overjoyed, dancing with rapturous joy. Jesus, the Messiah, had conquered death, hell and the grave. He had accomplished what the prophets had written. . . all in the space of three years. They remembered Him saying, "This is My commandment; that you love one another as I have loved you. No one has greater love than to lay down his own life for his friends. You are My friends if you keep on doing the things which I command you to do." (John 15:12, 13) "What love He has," they thought, "to die for us so we can live forever. We must be obedient to His word."

As the celebration calmed down, Jesus needed to complete His mission for the evening. "Peace to you! Just as the Father has sent Me. I also send you." When He had said this, Jesus breathed on them and said, "Receive the Holy Spirit. If you forgive the sins of any, they are forgiven them; if you retain the sins of any, they are retained." (John 20:22-23)

Jesus was completing the mission He came to earth to accomplish. When Jesus breathed on those in the room, they became new creatures in Christ Jesus. They became born again because they believed in who Jesus was. This couldn't have happened any earlier, even if they knew and believed Jesus was the Son of God because Jesus had not gone through the death, burial, and resurrection. Now that He had accomplished that, the disciples were renewed in spirit and truth. Today, when we hear, believe and accept the life and ministry of Jesus, we too can receive the indwelling of the Holy Spirit, the third part of the Trinity.

Not to be forgotten is the mandate that Jesus gave the disciples once they did receive the indwelling of the Holy Spirit and that is forgiveness. One of the lessons Jesus taught the disciples was on forgiveness. He said, "Whenever you are praying, if you have anything against anyone, forgive him, that your Father in Heaven may also forgive you your sins. But if you do not forgive, neither will your Father in Heaven forgive your sins." (Mark 11:25,26) Jesus

> **Forgiveness**
> *Freedom, pardon, deliverance, liberty*

knew that unforgiveness will hinder anyone's relationship with the Father and also hinder relationships with others. Unforgiveness is the opposite of love. When there is love, there is forgiveness.

Once Jesus had completed conveying His mandate to the disciples He left the same way He had come in to the room, through the wall. The men stood astonished and the night was filled with a new sense of expectation and excitement. Not all the disciples were present when Jesus was among them. Thomas was on an errand and upon returning got quite a heart-stopping report on what had transpired that evening. Thomas listened to what they had to say, but was quite reluctant to jump into believing such an outlandish story. He said, "Unless I see in His hands the print of the nails, and put my finger into those holes and put my hand into His side, I will not believe." (John 20:24, 25)

> **Believe**
> *Assurance, Confidence, Conviction*

About a week later, all the men, including Thomas had gathered together. Again, with the doors shut, Jesus just appeared among them and said, "Peace to you!" Looking around the room, He spotted Thomas and walked over to him. "Reach your finger here and look at My hands," He said as He extended His wrists toward Thomas. "Now bring your hand here," Jesus said as He lifted His robe to expose the wound on His side, "and put it into My side." Looking around the room, Jesus said, "Do not be unbelieving, but believing." Returning His gaze to Thomas, Jesus gently spoke and said, "Thomas, because you have seen Me, you have believed. Blessed are those who have not seen and yet have believed." (John 20:26-29)

> **Blessed**
> *A continuation of fortune and happiness*

Many of us find it hard to believe in anything we can't see with our own eyes. We are humans so God has given us eyes, ears, smell, taste and touch that we can be convicted or believe in someone or something. Faith doesn't require our senses, but does require a trust in someone or something without physical or sensual evidence. (Hebrews 11:1) Thomas needed to see and feel in order to believe that Jesus was really alive, but according to Jesus, those of us who cannot nor will not see Jesus physically and still believe that He is alive will be more blessed than the disciples.

CHAPTER 46

The 40-Day Walk

Once Jesus appeared to His disciples, He remained in the Jerusalem area for forty days, continuing to talk about the Kingdom of Heaven but not always just with the disciples. There were many followers that experienced Jesus' presence in that time. He performed many more miracles and signs so that they would believe that He was the Christ, the Son of God, and that believing not only they, but you may have life in His name. (John 20:30-31) There were many things that Jesus did, which if they were written one by one, even the world itself could not contain the books that would be written. (John 21:25)

The day finally came that Jesus needed to complete His task on earth. Jesus knew that the disciples and many others were ready to continue the work He had started. But they needed their "work orders" to activate them. He got word to the eleven disciples who were waiting for Him in Galilee to meet so He could give them their last instructions. It wouldn't be necessary for Him to remain on the earth because these eleven disciples and others were witnesses of His life. He had told them that it was necessary for the Christ to suffer and to rise from the dead the third day and that repentance and remission of sins should be preached in His name to all nations, beginning at Jerusalem.

As the men gathered with Jesus, they worshipped Him and glorified God. The disciples knew they would serve their Lord and Master for the rest of their lives. They were totally committed to sharing what they had witnessed to their friends and family. There were a few that doubted; not in whom Jesus was, but who they were. They doubted that they could be used; they doubted that they were able to do or speak the things of the Kingdom, but those doubts started to dissolve as Jesus began to speak. What Jesus was about to tell them changed not only their idea of their future, but their whole purpose in life

"All authority has been given to Me in Heaven and on earth. Now I am giving that authority to you. Go and make disciples of all the nations, baptizing them in the name of the Father and of the Son and of the Holy Spirit, teaching them to observe all things that I have commanded you. Do not be afraid, because I will always be with you, even to the end of the age." (Matthew 28:18-20)

Jesus reminded them what He had told them, 'The Holy Spirit will glorify Me, for He will take of what is Mine and declare it to you. All things that the Father has are Mine. Therefore I said that He will take of Mine and declare it to you.' (John 16:14,15) As that revelation filled their spirit, they realized that Jesus was giving them the same power and authority He carried with Him to them. They felt something was changing their outlook on life, their attitudes and ambition just through the power of Jesus' words. If He was going to be with them, they knew they would have the confidence to be world changers. They were receiving the Keys of the Kingdom.

Jesus continued, bringing them back to the present, saying "Go into all the world and preach this good news to every creature. He who believes and is baptized will be saved; but he who does not believe will be condemned. And these signs will follow those who

> **Saved**
> *Saved from sin, healed and delivered. Preserved, be made whole, and do well, protected*

believe: In My name they will cast out demons; they will speak with new tongues; they will take up serpents; and if they drink anything deadly, it will by no means hurt them; they will lay hands on the sick, and they will recover." (Mark 16:15-18)

> **Condemned**
> *Judged, condemned, damned, punished*

The disciples were leaning forward, listening to every word that came out of Jesus' mouth. They were amazed to hear what they were given authority to do. All these things defy the laws of nature and they didn't understand all of them. Even the men and women who had come from the poorest of homes, the smallest tribe, the ones who had been told all their lives they wouldn't amount to anything had just been told they were to teach and preach this Good News to everyone. Again, the doubts flooded back into their thoughts.

Jesus knew what they were thinking. "They are still thinking the thoughts of their fathers and the generations of men and women before them. On their own, they simply could not survive the thrusts and obstacles that Satan will throw at them. But when I am gone from the earth, the One to walk with them daily and empower each and every one of them will come." With that, Jesus said,

"Listen, I will send the Promise of My Father upon you, which you have heard from Me; for John truly baptized with water, but you shall be baptized with the Holy Spirit not many days from now." (Acts 1:4,5)

The disciples totally misunderstood the meaning of Jesus' statement. One of them asked "Lord, will You at this time restore the Kingdom to Israel?" Jesus patiently replied, "It is not for you to know times or seasons which the Father has put in His own authority, but you shall receive power when the Holy Spirit has come upon you; and you shall be witnesses to Me in Jerusalem, and in all Judea and Samaria, and to the end of the earth." (Acts 1:7, 8)

Again, Jesus was commissioning them to leave their families and homes and go to regions beyond their villages and towns. The news, the story of Jesus, was too important to keep to themselves, but they were going to need supernatural help. That was the gift Jesus was extending to them, but they had to obey Him and wait in Jerusalem until they were given the power needed to complete what Jesus required.

"Boldness," Jesus thought, "is what they will need and the Holy Spirit is the Person and the Power by which help and ability will be given. Once received, anyone will have the ability to serve, share the life and power of God's Kingdom with others, but that power must be received voluntarily and by faith."

Jesus knew this is not automatic like the indwelling of the Holy Spirit when one hears and accepts the Good News. Jesus continued to contemplate what will be next for the disciples and other followers. "Even My mother, Mary and the other women are going to need the help through the indwelling of the Holy Spirit," He thought. "Oh, those will be exciting days, but for now, I must say My goodbyes." Turning to the disciples closest to Him, He said, "Come, let us journey to Bethany."

Jesus talked with each disciple with a special word of encouragement and walked with them as far as Bethany. They stepped off the road where He blessed them. As He was speaking, Jesus was carried upward toward Heaven. Everyone watched in awe and amazement as He slowly lifted off the ground and floated upward. As He passed through the clouds two men appeared who were dressed in bright white garments said, "Men of Galilee, why do you stand gazing up into heaven? This same Jesus, who was taken up from you into Heaven, will so come in like manner as you saw

Him go into heaven." (Acts 1:9-11) The message was clear, quit gazing into an empty sky looking for something that isn't there. You have been given your orders; now go do what Jesus told you to do.

Epilogue

"Father, I'm home!" "Welcome, My Son, I've been waiting your arrival with great anticipation. I know the task was accomplished with great success and the atmosphere on the earth is already beginning to change. There is hope, anticipation and victory among a few, but in a few years that will begin to explode into a revival of hearts and minds all around the world.

"Your journey was well worth the cost, my Son", said the Father. "Satan has lost His dominion of savage and vile destruction, killing and stealing. Through the sacrifice of the shedding of Your innocent blood on a cross, all their sins have been redeemed back to Me. I can once again have a close relationship with all who will seek Me and accept what You did on the cross. My Son, You are worthy of all praise and adoration."

"You have put the Keys of the Kingdom back into the hands of My precious people. Now they have all the power and the authority it will take to overrule the wiles of their enemy. Even though you have destroyed the works of the devil, it will not be easy to retrain their thinking to recognize his tricks and deception, but there are people ready to take up the mantle of discipling and mentoring the new believers." The Father turned to face His Son and with a big grin gestured to the seat next to Him. "Jesus, will you sit at My right hand as the Triumphant One?

So then, after the Lord had spoken to them, He was received up into heaven, and sat down at the right hand of God. And they went out and preached everywhere, the Lord working with them and confirming the word through the accompanying signs. Amen. Mark 16:19, 20

Author's Note

Although this happened over 2,000 years ago, the message is still real and applicable to us today. Jesus died for You! He knew you would be born when you were born. He knew where you would be born and to the parents you were born. He has designed you for a specific purpose that only you can accomplish. Jesus loves you very much and wants to give you a wonderful life, however you have the choice. To choose Jesus Christ as your Lord and Savior, you will not only spend eternity with Him in Heaven, but He will walk with you through all your days on this earth.

Your other choice is to deny what you have read in this book. To pass Jesus off as another great teacher or a good man who lived 2,000 years ago. That is exactly what Satan wants you to think so you can spend eternity with him. The place he lives is so horrible that Jesus sacrificed Himself so you wouldn't have to dip one toe in that place of eternal torture.

If you would like to receive Jesus as your personal Savior, pray this prayer:

Oh God! I declare that I believe Jesus Christ is your Son and that He was born of a virgin 2,000 years ago. I believe He shed His blood so my sins might be forgiven. I believe You raised Him from the dead. I believe that Jesus is the only Way to the true and living God. Jesus is the only Way to receive eternal life. I believe that as I make Him the Lord and Master of my life, every work of the devil is broken in my life. I am free from the devil's bondage and free from sin. I declare that Satan is no longer my master, but that Your Son, Jesus Christ, is my Master from this day forward. I further declare that I will serve Him the rest of my life. Thank you Father, for sending your Son to die for me.

The Mystery Answered
(Ephesians 3:14-21)

For this reason, I bow my knees to the Father of our Lord Jesus Christ, from whom the whole family in heaven and earth is named, that He would grant you, according to the riches of His glory,

- to be strengthened with the might through His Spirit in the inner man,
- that Christ may dwell in your hearts through faith;
- that you, being rooted and grounded in love, may be able to comprehend with all the saints what is the width and length and depth and height to know the love of Christ which passes knowledge;
- that you may be filled with all the fullness of God.

Now to Him who is able to do exceedingly abundantly above all that we ask or think, according to the power that works in us, to Him be glory in the church by Christ Jesus to all generations, forever and ever. Amen.